Primo Time

Also by Antony Sher

Fiction

Middlepost
Indoor Boy
Cheap Lives
The Feast

Non-Fiction

Year of the King
Woza Shakespeare!
(*co-written with Greg Doran*)
Beside Myself

Stage Play

I.D.

TV Filmscript

Changing Step

Paintings and Drawings

Characters

Antony Sher

PRIMO TIME

NICK HERN BOOKS
London
www.nickhernbooks.co.uk

A Nick Hern Book

Primo Time first published as a paperback original in 2005
in Great Britain by Nick Hern Books Ltd, 14 Larden Road,
London W3 7ST, and in South Africa by Pan Macmillan,
2nd Floor, North Block, Hyde Park Corner, Johannesburg.

Quotations from Primo Levi's *If This Is A Man* and
The Truce are from the English translation by Stuart Woolf
published by Abacus, a division of Time Warner Books, in 1987

Typeset by Country Setting, Kingsdown, Kent CT14 8ES
Printed and bound in Great Britain by Biddles, King's Lynn

British Library Cataloguing Data for this book is available
from the British Library

ISBN 1 85459 852 X

In memory of Primo Levi, 1919–1987

Acknowledgements

My thanks to Nick Hern, who has been exceptionally good to work with, both as publisher and editor; and to the four people who read the manuscript of this book, and helped to guide its progress: Greg Doran, Mic Cheetham, Paul Lyon-Maris, and Richard Wilson.

A.S.

Contents

Primo Time

Part One

Writing Primo

Saturday 2nd November 2002

I wonder if Nelson Mandela knows Primo Levi?

As a writer, I mean. Mandela was an avid reader in prison, but would his jailers have allowed Levi's works? Several of them are like handbooks on how to endure cruelty. Mandela and Levi have much in common. Both experienced brutal incarcerations. Both survived with inspiring strength. Both returned to freedom imbued with a spirit of forgiveness rather than revenge.

The reason they're linked in my mind is because I'm about to see Mandela in person – I'm in a taxi on the way to South Africa House – and I'm currently thinking about adapting Primo Levi's book, *If This Is A Man,* for the stage.

I first read *If This Is A Man,* in which Levi describes his year in Auschwitz, when I was rehearsing Peter Flannery's *Singer* at the RSC in 1989. Peter Flannery had used Levi's book as his research for the first scene of the play, and urged us all to look at it. It immediately became a very important book for me. Levi takes you by the hand and says, Come let me guide you through hell. You see, smell, taste it. The detail is astonishing. Levi was a chemist by profession, and he somehow maintained a calm and analytical view of existence in Auschwitz even though he was in mortal danger. He described it like this: 'I was constantly pervaded by a curiosity . . . the curiosity of the naturalist who finds himself transported into an environment that is monstrous but new, monstrously new'. It isn't just the detail though. It's the compassion, the wisdom. He's in a mad, senseless situation, yet instead of recording it with anger and bitterness, he somehow forgives it; he knows it is *human*. The SS are not from Mars; they're us.

And that's why Mandela could be Levi's brother or comrade. His oppressors were almost as crazy as the SS, and yet when Mandela advocated reconciliation rather than revenge, he was forcing us to remember that these people were not from Mars either. In fact, the Afrikaners who cooked up apartheid had been the victims just a few decades earlier: the second-class citizens in British South Africa, the vanquished in the Anglo-Boer War (during which the British invented the concentration camp).

The taxi reaches South Africa House. Home from home for me. I often had to report here when I first came to London from Cape Town in 1968. It was a grim and ugly place then, a sinister fortress, a symbol of the old regime. Nowadays I come here to party. Today's will celebrate the tenth anniversary of the publication of Mandela's *Long Walk To Freedom*, and the great man himself has flown into town. My partner Greg (Doran, RSC Associate Director) and I are among the lucky ones invited along.

All the usual suspects are in the first-floor reception room: the High Commissioner of course, Lindiwe Mabuza – a radiant, big-hearted woman, a poetess in her spare time – her deputy George Johannes, the writers Gillian Slovo and Anthony Sampson, the actress Janet Suzman, and my friend Ethel de Keyser (who runs the Canon Collins Educational Trust for Southern Africa), buzzing around as she always does, introducing us all to one another, sniffing the air for potential sponsors and donors. A few surprises too. Robert McBride is here. These days he's an MP in South Africa, but previously he was in the ANC miltary wing, Umkhonto we Sizwe, and personally responsible for the Magoo's Bar bombing in Durban in 1986, which killed 3 people and injured another 89. He was on Death Row for years, and after his release I interviewed him for my Death Row novel, *Cheap Lives*. Quite a difficult customer then – troubled and defensive. I'm rather surprised when he recognises me today and greets me warmly.

We're all chatting away, when there's a sudden, unmistakable hush. Mandela has come in. You can't see him yet – just the crowd surrounding him. He slowly emerges into view as he's ushered up a ramp onto the raised platform at the Trafalgar Square end of the room. He's wearing one of his trademark high-collared African shirts, in black and gold, and although he uses a stick to get to his chair, he abandons it when he moves to the lectern. He looks thinner than when we last saw him this close – during the Celebrate South Africa events in 2001 – but is imbued with unexpected playfulness. Begins by telling us that the phenomenal sales for *Long Walk* indicate a terrible drop in literary standards in the West. We laugh, and from now on we're his. He talks for about half an hour, without notes. In a way he rambles slightly, like old men do, yet every diversion holds a fascinating anecdote. The original draft of his book was smuggled out of his cell on Robben Island – 'I can't tell you how, or they might lock me up again.' His stories have surprising details – very human, very Primo Levi – like how nervous he felt when, on a secret visit from prison in 1989, he had his first meeting with F.W. de Klerk: 'He came striding out of a door which I took to be an office, but which, when I became President myself, I learned was a loo.' He talks of how both de Klerk and Bush (Senior) chided him for his friendships with Gaddafi, Castro and Khomeni, and asked him to renounce them. He refused, with a classic piece of Mandela-ese: 'If I drop them, my old friends, to please you, my new friends, you'd

never trust me again. If I can do it to them, I can do it to you.'
I lean forward as he talks of his struggle to reconcile rather
than revenge: 'If we listened to our blood – and our blood was
boiling – the country would've gone up in flames.'

Extraordinary though. How do you resist the primal instinct
to strike back when you're hurt? Primo Levi asks an opposite
question when they're about to board the transport to Auschwitz, and they receive the first blows: 'How can one man hit
another without anger?'

Mandela finishes by chatting about his new wife, Graça
Machel. He tells us that she's the powerful one now, and he's
just an unemployed old man. 'People ask me why I allowed her
to keep her former surname. I tell them the miracle is that she
allowed me to keep mine!'

As he finishes, I turn to Janet Suzman next to me: 'I realise
I've been smiling for about half an hour now, and my face is
quite sore.' She beams: 'Yes, he's just so . . . good!'

He's helped down the ramp. People flock round to shake his
hand, just to touch him. Greg and I met him during the
Celebrate South Africa festivities, and, face to face, his presence
is remarkable, his sense of serenity; you carry it away with you
like a gift. 'I don't think we need join the throng again today,'
says Greg; 'Just being here is enough.' I say, 'OK', while
thinking: *Pity, I wanted to ask if he knows Primo Levi.*

Thursday 7th November 2002

Grayshott Hall Health Farm. Been here for five days with
Richard (Wilson, actor and director), thoroughly indulging our-
selves. This is my treat at the end of a year of hard work: with
the RSC, in Greg's season of Jacobethan plays at the Swan in
Stratford. In between all the treatments, saunas and massages,
Richard and I have taken long walks across the open shrub-
land beyond Grayshott's property. During these expeditions,
I've felt rather relieved that *One Foot In The Grave* is no longer

on; at the height of its popularity you couldn't go anywhere with Richard – not even this quiet heath – without people staring, waving, stopping to chat. Richard and I have been best friends for thirty years, and although his new, super-star fame was a wonderful thing (coming quite late in his career, it can serve as an inspiration to all frustrated actors), I never got used to sharing his company with the rest of the nation.

Today we were planning a walk, but the weather turned grey and wet, and we were confined to quarters. After lunch, I came back to my room for a snooze, but instead found myself sitting at the window, staring out at the drizzle, doing some stock-taking. Both my careers, acting and writing, feel as though they're in some trouble at the moment.

The Jacobethans have been remarkaby successful – five unknown classical pieces won rave reviews and played to packed houses – and I've felt proud of my own contribution, as Domitian Caesar in *The Roman Actor* and the title role in *The Malcontent*. But at the same time I've been nursing a secret problem. Stage fright. This first started while I was in Recovery from cocaine addiction in 1996, but it seems to be getting steadily worse now. Apparently it's not uncommon as actors get older. Olivier had it so badly while he was running the National that he had to instruct the company never to meet his eyes while they were onstage with him. For me, during the Jacobethans, this thing that I've dubbed The Fear has been quite merciless. Practically every performance is done to the accompaniment of three babbling voices: the first is my own, speaking the lines, the second is an inner demon, telling me I'm going to fuck up, and the third is an inner angel, telling the demon to fuck off. The inside of my head gets quite noisy. At times it's intolerable. I'm seriously thinking about giving up acting – theatre acting. Maybe doing an occasional film or TV, but mainly writing full-time. Except there's a problem here too . . .

I've just heard that Hutchinson is doing nothing to promote the paperback of my autobiography, *Beside Myself.* While my editor Paul Sidey was away on sick leave, they seem to have made some corporate decision to abandon the book. It's not commercial, and that's all the big publishers care about these days. I made several suggestions about publicising it – a leaflet in the RSC mailing list, an advert in the programme when the Jacobethans transfer to London – but these things would cost money, and they're not prepared to fork out anything at all, apparently. Since this particular book is rather special to me, the news has really shocked me.

Writing has become an addiction for me, and I have to find a way of feeding my habit. I've grown disheartened with writing novels: they didn't find much of a readership, and in the end, one way or the other, I seem to need an audience. So might stage plays be the answer? My first, *I.D.*, is already written, and will be performed at the Almeida next autumn. It's exciting, but a long time to wait. Since productions seem to take forever to set up, I need to get another play on the go.

So what about Primo Levi then?

Mic (Cheetham, Literary Agent) says there could be difficulties getting the rights – from the Levi family and the translators – and since we've just been through all of this with *I.D.* (also based on a book, Henk van Woerden's *A Mouthful of Glass*), she says couldn't I just write an original play instead?

But the Primo Levi idea just won't go away. I've brought my Abacus paperback to Grayshott. It's a combined edition of *If This Is A Man* and *The Truce,* the account of his journey home after Auschwitz. I would only want to do the first book.

You couldn't turn it into a conventional play. In fact, I don't believe it's possible to put Auschwitz on stage, or indeed screen, in any conventional manner. Not even *Schindler's List* convinced me. And on the two occasions I played concentration camp inmates myself – in *Singer*'s first scene, and the TV film *Genghis Cohen* – shaving my head and donning the striped uniform, I felt deeply uncomfortable. Me, a free and well-fed man, pretending to be in the Lager, acting it out – no, there was something unacceptable here. The author Gitta Sereny, who's written biographies of Albert Speer and Franz Stangl (commandant of Treblinka), has said of the Holocaust that it's too soon for art, and I half agree with her. But might it be possible to do *If This Is A Man* as Primo Levi's testimony? Levi in post-war mode, like the famous photo of him lifting his glasses: brushed hair, grey beard, shirt and tie. As though he were one of the survivors interviewed in the Holocaust documentary, *Shoah*. Its director, Claude Lanzmann, took a brave but admirable decision. He never shows the newsreel footage of the camps. He stays in the present day, and although he accompanies some of his interviewees back to the sites of their imprisonment, he prompts them to just talk, just tell us what happened. He knows their stories are enough. He knows that word pictures can be more powerful than the other kind. *Shoah* lasts eight hours, during which Lanzmann asks the viewer to simply watch different people telling us about their experiences; recognisable modern people filmed in colour, not the walking skeletons in grainy monochrome which we've seen so many times we've almost become hardened and indifferent, as we sometimes are to images of famine victims in Africa. Lanzmann says to his audience, don't think of this as being about 'them', think of it as 'us'. And the result is devastating.

Couldn't you do the same with Primo Levi's account? He's regarded as one of the most eloquent witnesses to the Holocaust. Wouldn't it be fascinating to have *him* tell us about it? Or an illusion of him. Something halfway between documentary and art.

Which means, I suppose, a one-man show. And, I suppose, me doing it. It would be very strange if I adapted the book in this way, and then didn't perform it.

So the big question is this: if you're currently suffering from chronic stage fright, is it a good idea to write yourself a one-man show?

Friday 8th November 2002

Oh sod it, I'm going for it. Never mind the *performing* of the thing – and actually Henry Goodman would be terrific in the part – I'm just going to try *writing* it for now. I'm not even convinced it can work, so I'll just do it as an experiment. Then if it's OK I could offer it to the Holocaust Educational Trust (I'm on their board) as a piece for next year's January 27th event – Holocaust Day – as some kind of private performance maybe. And then if that's OK, we can sort out the rights and all the other official bollocks. I know it's a crazy way round, but I don't care. I woke up this morning and knew I was going to do it. The opening line of the book was going round and round in my head:

'It was my good fortune to be deported to Auschwitz only in 1944 . . .'

He goes on to explain there was a shortage of labour by then, so the Nazis extended the average lifespan of the prisoners in the camps. But the line is deliberately provocative, and grabs the reader straightaway. It would have the same effect on an audience. What a way to start:

'It was my good fortune to be deported to Auschwitz . . .'

Monday 11th November 2002

Been writing non-stop for days now, from about 4am to 9pm – back in London – with Greg bringing meals down to the study. I'm in a kind of fever. Primo Levi talks of something similar when he takes the chemistry exam in Auschwitz (his camp, Monowitz, was attached to the Buna rubber factory, where they had a laboratory): 'This excitement which I feel warm in my veins, I recognise it, it's the fever of examinations, *my* fever of *my* examinations.' Writing any piece is like an exam; will you do justice to your subject, will you live up to the moment of being tested? If the answer feels more yes than no, then it becomes an exquisite fever. Primo's chemistry exam is an example of something I'd forgotten about in the book: at times it's like Kafka, or Swift, or even Lewis Carroll; a journey through a lunatic world. The exam is a matter of life and death for Primo – he's not surviving well in the camp, and will perish unless he becomes a specialist worker in a more sheltered environment – yet he has to take it in German, a language he barely speaks, and when it's over, the applicants hear no results (not till months later). It's crazy. Like the distribution of food and clothes – you need a slave army, yet you starve and freeze them – and like the little band which plays popular songs as the skeletal prisoners march to and from work. Levi describes the band as 'the voice of the Lager, the perceptible expression of its geometric madness' , and he describes the prisoners with the curious beauty that pervades the book: 'The dance of the dead men.'

Tuesday 12th November 2002

Two big biographies of Primo Levi came out earlier this year, by Carole Angier and Ian Thomson. I'm finding it useful to compare their material with the events in *If This Is A Man*. Trouble is, there's extra detail that tempts me. It's mostly from Levi himself, from his later writing, when he returns to the subject in *The Truce, Moments of Reprieve, The Periodic Table* and *The Drowned and the Saved*. Should I use some of this?

It's been a surprise to learn that Primo Levi, widely regarded as a great Jewish figure, was non-practising and non-believing – both before the war, and even more so afterwards, when he wrote, 'There was Auschwitz, therefore God cannot exist.' There's a striking moment at the beginning of *If This Is A Man*, when, as a member of a small, almost amateur partisan band, he's arrested by the Italian Fascist Militia, and interrogated. He has to choose between declaring his political beliefs or his Jewish race. He's between a rock and a hard place, but he thinks it's safer to identify himself as Jewish . . . ! Being a

secular Jew myself, I feel even more intrigued by him than
before.

While I was working away today, Nancy Meckler left a message on the answerphone about the casting of *I.D.* (which she's
directing). The play is about the 1966 assassination of the South
African Prime Minister, Hendrik Verwoerd, by a mixed-race
oddball named Demetrios Tsafendas. When we did one of the
readings of it at the National Theatre Studio, Simon Russell
Beale was exceptionally good as Tsafendas, and we've been
waiting for months to hear if he'll play it in the actual production. Apparently he's trying to decide between us and a revival
of *Jumpers* at the National. I bumped into him the other day
and said, 'A choice between Sher and Stoppard – no contest
surely?' I don't think he realised I was joking – he didn't smile.
Anyway, he's chosen Stoppard now, and we can't think of anyone else to play the part, which is of the ultimate outsider.
Today, Nancy's message went: 'Look Tony, I've been thinking
. . . it seems odd leaving this on your machine, but . . . I think
you should play Tsafendas.' Later, Mike (Attenborough,
Almeida Artistic Director) also rang to endorse the idea.

Dear God, here I am trying to use playwrighting as a way of
acting less, and it's somehow doing the opposite. In all the
Studio workshops and readings of *I.D.* I did no acting at all,
and thoroughly enjoyed the experience – just being the
playwright. But the idea of me as Tsafendas has always been
held as a fallback plan, and now it looks like I might have to do
it. The situation is getting too nerve-wracking otherwise. Because we're also waiting on Richard E. Grant, who was splen-
did as Verwoerd in another of the readings – funny, chilling,
and, because of his Swaziland upbringing, able to do the accent.
He says he's keen to play it, but he's about to direct his first
film, and the dates might clash. He wants Ralph Fiennes – as
do his backers – but Ralph isn't sure he's available. So Richard
is waiting on Ralph, and we're waiting on Richard. Bloody
actors.

Thursday 14th November 2002

Writing, writing, writing. This could work! My prejudices about one-man shows are slipping away. Paring down the book – and I'm remaining very faithful to Levi's own words – it becomes a Beckett-like monologue; instead of the character being buried in sand, he's trapped in Auschwitz. (During the chemistry exam, when he finds himself in a spotless office, he comes up with a very Beckettian line: 'I would leave a stain on whatever I touched.') I think the piece should have that kind of stark stillness. I'm writing practically no stage directions: just occasionally, 'he stands, he sits'. With material as intense and harrowing as this, the slightest movement could be powerful. Richard (Wilson) would be the perfect director. One of his favourite words is minimalism.

Friday 15th November 2002

Well, I've sort of finished. My exquisite fever has lasted exactly a week, raging round the clock, all day, every day. I'd always thought of *If This Is A Man* as quite a slender book, but it isn't, and cutting it down to about one-and-a-half hour's playing time (36 pages at the moment) has been difficult. In crude terms, I've concentrated on action and character, and lost some of the philosophy. For example, one of the most famous chapters is 'The Canto of Ulysses', in which the Italian Primo tries to recount an episode from Dante's *Inferno* to another prisoner who only speaks French. It's about the healing power of art in desperate circumstances, rather like the copy of Shakespeare, disguised as the Koran, which was kept by Mandela and the other prisoners on Robben Island. Well, I've cut 'Canto of Ulysses' entirely. This will upset some people, but it's simply too literary, too inactive for what I'm trying to create. Levi's writing is so detailed – and this is what makes him special as a witness – that if you want certain sequences to have their proper weight, you have to lose others altogether.

In the last few days, I've sifted through the whole piece again, inserting the stories of Lorenzo and Alberto. How could I have left them out? They are the heart and soul of the piece. They both save Primo's life. Lorenzo through practical help, Alberto through friendship. Lorenzo is a bricklayer, one of the civilian workers building the rubber factory at Auschwitz, who, as a fellow Italian, smuggled extra food to Primo. Alberto is a prisoner who arrived on the same transport as Primo. He's also a chemist, about the same age, with similar build and looks; people get them confused and just call them 'the two Italians' or 'the twins'. In the Lager, everyone is alone, Primo tells us, 'desperately and ferociously alone', but he and Alberto link up, sharing every scrap of food they scavenge beyond the ration. They're conducting an experiment – a chemical experiment in a way – is there not more strength in two? They succeed right until the end, when Primo falls ill with scarlet fever, and can't join the evacuation march when the Germans flee Auschwitz. This turns into the *Todesmarsch*, the Death March, during which about 20,000 prisoners perish, including Alberto. I find this moment in the book unbearable. Primo loses his twin, and twins have always been important to me. Maybe because I'm Geminian. Maybe because Greg is a real twin. (As is my first partner, Jim Hooper.)

The ending of *Primo* is still a worry. (I'm calling it *Primo* – the only thing I don't like about *If This Is A Man* is the title, which is somehow both mysterious and portentous.) At the moment I have the actor come out of character and tell us about Primo Levi's shocking death in 1987 – falling down the stairwell of his apartment block in Turin – and speculate on the different explanations, leaving it as an open question:

Was it suicide? At the time, the newspapers said: *Auschwitz Claims Him Forty Years Later*. He was a depressive all his life; it was a clinical condition.

Was it an accident? He was under heavy medication (for depression), and may have fainted, toppling over the bannister.

As a chemist, if he wanted to commit suicide, he had access to methods which were less painful and more reliable: he fell only three floors.

Was it murder? By Neo-Nazis.

I'm not sure any of this belongs in *Primo*. But anyway I can decide later. In the meantime I feel elated. I've written another play. Well no, it's not strictly a play. More just an adaptation. Or really just an abridgement. Anyway, whatever it is, *Primo* now exists.

Saturday 16th November 2002

An odd thing happened this morning. Any new piece of writing always goes straight to Greg for his opinion. But when I asked him to look at this first rough draft, he suggested that I read it aloud to him instead: 'It's written for one voice, so let me hear it like that.' I hesitated for a long moment, then agreed. We went up to his study. The reading was not good. Mainly because I couldn't get through certain sections without crying – particularly anything to do with Alberto – and this was both absurd and wrong. The one thing Primo never does is cry. If this had been an audition, I would've failed. At the end, when I finally looked up at Greg, his face was also wet with tears. 'We're just a pair of sentimental old poofs,' he said, breaking into laughter.

'The timing was one hour forty,' I said: 'But since about ten minutes of that was crying time, it's about right.'

Tears aside, we were both encouraged by the reading. We treated ourselves to lunch at Islington's new Italian restaurant, Metrogusto, and talked on. Greg definitely felt it could work, and that Richard was the man to direct it – it was somehow understood, without a word, that it should be Richard rather than him.

The discussion was so engrossing, it was only afterwards I remembered I don't have the rights to *If This Is A Man*, and that Mic reckons they could be seriously difficult to get. This is more worrying now – now that the piece seems to have potential.

Sunday 17th November 2002

Following yesterday's conversation with Greg, I change the ending of *Primo*. The surprising thing about *If This Is A Man* is that it's curiously uplifting; it's about survival not destruction. So I've cut any mention of Levi's death. Instead I describe the train journey when he finally reaches Italy again after Auschwitz (an echo of the transport in the opposite direction which begins the piece). This is borrowed from *The Truce*. Then I borrow a section from *The Periodic Table*, the book in which Levi brings together his twin careers as writer and chemist. In the last chapter, 'Carbon', he shows how matter changes. An atom of carbon enters the leaf of a tree, then the trunk, then a woodworm, and so on . . . eventually a glass of milk, which is drunk by the author himself, and the book finishes as he guides his hand 'to impress on the paper this dot, here, this one.' In the same way, Levi transforms the horror of Auschwitz into the power of *If This Is A Man*. And so *Primo* can end with him saying the first line again: 'It was my good fortune to be deported to Auschwitz . . . '

Monday 18th November 2002

Meeting with Nick Hytner (Artistic Director of the National Theatre). Similar to the one I had a few weeks ago with Mike Grandage, who's just taken over the Donmar. While struggling to decide whether to give up theatre, I'm also doing the opposite: putting myself about, trying to convey that I don't work exclusively for the RSC. My new fear about acting isn't helped by my intense association with a company currently being battered from every possible angle, both inside and out.

The only polite thing to say about Adrian Noble's reforms, the so-called Project Fleet, is that he's done the honourable thing and resigned. But the press love bad news in the arts, and love making it worse. The anti-RSC bias is preposterous. Every year the arts correspondents gleefully report that the National has just received ninety-nine nominations in the Olivier Awards, and the RSC none at all. No-one ever asks if this is just. Have we really done no exceptional work in the last few years? I think we have. No, this is just prejudice, just ridiculous. Neverthelss, the constant negativity is wearing me down, and, though I'll never leave the RSC, I need to do what every other actor does, and freelance more.

Nick is an extremely neat, calm and contained individual – as two gay Jewish men, we couldn't be more different – and his plans for the National are inspiring to listen to: a whole season of plays with £10 tickets, for example. By chance I had photo-copied *Primo* this morning, and a spare script was pulsing away in my briefcase under the table. Toyed with the idea of asking Nick to read it, but changed my mind when he said one of his new policies was to stop doing small-cast plays with well-known actors in the Cottesloe. Let the Royal Court do these. The NT was somewhere writers could do big plays.

Maybe *Primo* is meant for the Court. Before lunch, I biked a copy to Richard, who's an Associate Director there. If he likes the script, I'm sure he'll feel a natural loyalty to show it to them.

Tuesday 19th November 2002

Mic has read *Primo*, and was very affected by it. She's going to try applying for the rights from the Primo Levi Estate, which is made up of his widow, Lucia, and his two grown-up children, Lisa and Renzo. Apparently you apply through Levi's publishers, Einaudi, in Turin. Mic will just present them with the idea for now, not the actual script. (I'm not supposed to

have written that yet.) And the Chairman of the Holocaust
Educational Trust, Greville Janner – Lord Janner – is penning
a covering letter, a kind of 'reference' for me, since they won't
have any idea who I am.

After the flurry of calls with Mic today, I become troubled.
The very word 'Estate' sends a chill through me. I've not had
good experiences with 'Estates'. When I did *Arturo Ui* at the
National, the Brecht Estate forbade us from using the best
translation, by George Tabori, because it adapts (and *improves* on)
the original. When I did Pam Gem's *Stanley* at the National, the
Stanley Spencer Estate forbade the reproduction of any paintings
under their control, which is about 97% of his total output.

The Spencer case is especially telling, and worrying. The
'Estate' is the painter's two daughters. And the families of
famous people don't always acknowledge the fact that their dad
or hubby has become public property, and that people are
going to write about them, discussing not only their work but
their private lives. Spencer's daughters took against Pam's play
because of the inclusion of his second, crazy, unconsummated
marriage to the lesbian Patricia Preece, after he'd deserted their
mother Hilda. In their version of his life, they'd prefer to leave
it out. But how could Pam Gems?

Then I half-remember something . . . isn't there a previous
stage version of *If This Is A Man*? Doesn't Carole Angier
mention it in her biography? When I read it, I made notes.
Leafing through them now, I find:

In 1962, a Canadian radio play of *If This Is A Man* . . . PL
likes it . . . writes his own version for Italian radio . . . they
record scenes outdoors . . . an Italian village where people
still wear clogs; the roads sound like the roads of
Auschwitz . . . much praised when broadcast.

Summer '64, agrees to a stage play of *I.T.I.A.M.* Writes
it with the young actor who played Alberto in radio version, Pieralberto Marche. They lessen the PL narrative

position – Primo is called Aldo – they argue about a Chorus, the Tower of Babel . . . 53 actors rehearse (from Italy, Germany, France, Israel, Poland, Hungary, all speaking their own languages) . . . the play's meant to open in Florence . . . devastated by a flood (4/11/64) . . . the cast lose cars and most possessions . . . everyone moves to Turin . . . show opens 19/11/64 . . . PL at opening with Lucia . . . what did he feel? . . . standing ovation . . . bad reviews . . . the only praise is for some of the abstract scenes: the marches, almost dances, to the Auschwitz band.

C.Angier concludes: The reality of Auschwitz could not be rendered on a stage.

I agree. I'm surprised PL thought differently.

But surely there's hope here? If a stage version already exists, and if PL co-wrote it, and enjoyed the whole process, surely his family will be open to the idea of another one?

Wednesday 20th November 2002

Richard rings. He's not a man known for idle praise, so it's a nice surprise to hear him say, 'It's wonderful.' He confesses he doesn't know the book, but says the script has given him the closest sensation he's ever had of Auschwitz. Thinks it should be the Court downstairs: 'It needs a big picture . . . a lone man in a big space . . . no set . . . just the best lighting designer in the world.' Says it's also overcome his aversion to one-man shows, which of course I share. I said, 'Let's just talk about casting for a moment – I want to avoid doing this myself, so I was thinking Henry Goodman could be terrific. Or Alan Corduner. What d'you think?' Richard did one of his stern silences, then said, 'What?! But you have to do it yourself. Of course you do. Don't be stupid.' His certainty made me laugh. I put down the phone feeling excited – and scared.

Friday 22nd November 2002

A breakthrough, I think. Ronnie (Harwood, playwright and cousin) has recruited help from the author Paul Bailey, who wrote the Introduction to *If This Is A Man* in the Abacus edition, and who knows the Levi family, and will try and contact them on our behalf. I sent a letter to Bailey today:

> . . . My literary agent, Mic Cheetham, has already spoken to Carmen Zuilli at Einaudi, Levi's publishers, and has been warned that the family are 'difficult'. I think you may have said something similar to Ronnie. Well, my feeling is *good* – they're right to be very, very protective of his work. The flesh crawls at the thought of what some people might do with the material, particularly in terms of 'dramatisations' . . .
>
> . . . My plan is to create the simplest of one-man performances: Levi in later life, neatly dressed, trimmed beard, spectacles – no striped Lager uniform artfully dirtied – just a man alone in a light, telling his story . . .
>
> . . . At the same time as you approach the family, Mic Cheetham and I will be making a formal approach to Carmen Zuilli at Einaudi . . .

Saturday 23rd November 2002

Greg and I went to the British Museum to see a new Antony Gormley piece, *Field For The British Isles*. It's breathtaking. A whole room is filled with little terracotta people. Thousands of them, spilling behind pillars and round corners and out of view. Their slightly different sizes and shades – some are fired yellowish, some red, some charcoal – make for a rolling landscape of people, all staring up as you peer in from the doorway. Their mass gaze carries a sense of expectancy. They want something from you. Is it help? It's comic at first, then poignant, then frightening . . . it could be an aerial view of Auschwitz.

Sunday 24th November 2002

Greg's birthday. I used an Antony Gormley picture as my card. We lunched at the Almeida Restaurant, sitting at a window, gazing at the building site across the road which will become the Almeida theatre again. I hope. The massive renovation is badly behind schedule. How do builders get away with never completing on time? Mike Attenborough told us a good story about this. When he complained to one of the head men a few months ago, the man replied shamelessly, 'It's alright, work should pick up now that Ireland's out of the World Cup.'

I felt quietly anxious all day. While everything goes quiet on the *Primo* front, it's a return to acting tomorrow – we start rehearsals for the Jacobethans in London. Will that mean a return of The Fear as well?

In the afternoon, I rang Mom in Cape Town. I asked about the weather. She said, 'It's very hot, which is odd, given it's our winter.' I frowned to myself – it's summer there – but said nothing. Told her we were counting the days to our Christmas holiday with them, and an escape from the grey skies here. She said, 'Oh that's odd, given it's your summer.'

Finished the call feeling troubled. My siblings are increasingly worried about Mom. They say it's more than just old age. Today was the day I felt they were right.

Monday 25th November 2002

RSC Rehearsal Rooms, Clapham. Whatever my worries about The Fear, it's a wonderful thing that we're all here today: 28 actors, 5 directors, teams of musicians and stage management. We stand beaming at one another. We did it. We got the season to London.

This wasn't easy – after Adrian Noble had the bright idea of making the RSC homeless in this city. I sat in his office one day, begging him to find a way of transferring the Jacobethans before he left as Artistic Director. I reminded him that when he first got the job, he'd said that the RSC ofen squandered its best work: didn't run or revive those productions enough. The Jacobethans had been one of the biggest successes of recent years. How could we just ditch it? He was sympathetic but punchdrunk by then – battered by the failure of Project Fleet – and said there was simply no money for it; we were lost unless we could find 'an angel', and he didn't know who that might be. After Adrian departed, Mike Boyd inherited so many problems that neither he nor anyone else in the organisation were any more hopeful about transferring the Jacobethans. Everyone maintained that the financial demands were prohibitive. Greg, who conceived and produced the season, was in despair. 'It isn't a question of how can we afford to do it,' he raged; 'How can we afford *not* to do it?' In the end it was Paul Lyon-Maris, my agent (as an actor), who got so pissed off with the situation that he picked up the phone himself and started ringing round producers. Almost immediately he found the perfect one, the 'angel' that Adrian had said was our only hope. Thelma Holt. Her style is best summed up by the answer she gave when someone asked why she wanted to bring five obscure classical plays into the West End: 'Darling, because it's impossible!' She recruited another generous and adventurous spirit, Bill Kenwright, and together with Greg they set about trying to make some difficult sums work. Last minute deadlines and crisis meetings followed one another in quick succession. Would every actor agree to go onto a flat rate? Would any theatre owner in Shaftesbury Avenue risk this particular season? Each time – by the skin of our teeth – the answer was yes. The Gielgud Theatre was secured, and a repertoire of the plays scheduled for an initial run of six weeks, with another six as a possible extension.

A miracle, a bloody miracle.

Monday 2nd December 2002

Ronnie has asked his Italian translator, Alessandra Serra, if she has any contacts who can help with the Primo Levi Estate. He passed on this reply from her today:

> Primo Levi's family are not only difficult, but impossible. This is what I was told. There is a man at Einaudi who might be of help. His name is Roberto Gilodi. He speaks English. I don't know him, but Paolo Collo, your and Harold (Pinter)'s publisher at Einaudi, gave me his name.

The first sentence is a shock. And yet oddly enough, as I said in my letter to Paul Bailey the other day, I approve. I want them to be difficult, I want them to be impossible, I want them to reject all proposals to stage or film the book in a conventional way. (Imagine what Hollywood might do with it!) But I also want them to realise that I'm not going to do that; I'm not going to cheapen Primo Levi, I'm not going to betray him.

I ring Mic. She doesn't think we can approach this man Roberto Gilodi until we've heard back from our contact at Einaudi, Carmen Zuilli, who is considering our application.

Mic advises me to sit tight, to be patient – but this isn't in my nature, and she knows it (we've been close friends for twenty years). I mean, why haven't I heard back from Paul Bailey yet? It's ten days since I wrote to him.

Thursday 5th December 2002

First preview of *The Malcontent* at the Gielgud. I made the mistake of peeking out at the audience beforehand. They were small. About 200 in a house that seats 900. I'd been warned, but I just didn't need to see it. A small West End audience always looks cold, huddled in little separate groups, and vaguely cross. *Why have you brought us to this dismal place?* In fact, in his pre-show pep talk, Dominic (Cooke, director) did a very good riff on the difference between Stratford and London audiences:

'In Stratford they've arrived an hour early, they're sitting on lovely sunlit grass with a view of the river, they're sipping Chardonnay, they're with friends, they stroll into the theatre, and if it's the Swan it's the loveliest theatre on earth. In London, they've dashed from work, they've been squashed on the tube, they've jostled up steep escalators, they've emerged into the sordid garbage and racket of the West End, they've finally plonked themselves down in a friendless, half-empty auditorium, and then they say through gritted teeth: *OK – entertain me!*'

And so the show proceeded. Laughs which had rocked the Swan disappeared altogether. I was neither uplifted by the sheer achievement of getting the Jacobethans to London nor plagued by The Fear. Instead, I just felt the grim reality of playing the West End with a non-commercial piece. One explanation for the missing laughs was provided afterwards by a friend of Amanda (Drew, actress), who reported that he was laughing heartily when a woman turned round and went, 'Shh!' This is another reason why the RSC needs its own London home. So it can have its own London audience. Who understand that the classics can be funny.

I never thought I'd say this, but tonight I missed the Barbican.

Saturday 7th December 2002

This card arrived from Paul Bailey this morning:

Many aplogies for the delay in replying. I don't know if Ronnie told you, but I'm trying to contact Levi's sister, Anna Maria, as I think she's your only hope as far as the Estate is concerned. Huge offence has been taken by the family re the two biographies – especially Carole Angier's.

I have asked a mutual friend to get in touch with her. To be perfectly honest, I don't hold out too much hope. Some years ago I met – and was charmed by – the film director Francesco Rosi, who made a movie of *La tregua* (*The Truce*). Perhaps your agent might think of contacting him? He is very simpatico.

Oh God, here we go. The 'Estate'. The family. They're unhappy with the biographies. What don't they like? The discussion of his death? (Both Angier and Thomson think it was suicide.) Or maybe of his home life? (It was troubled, apparently.) But how could biographers omit such things? I suppose that isn't the family's problem. Primo Levi may be the great Holocaust witness to us, but to them he's just a husband and father.

Is he public property? Is he ours or is he theirs?

Both.

This isn't looking good . . .

Thursday 12th December 2002

Gielgud Theatre. We start the tech (the technical rehearsal) of *The Roman Actor*. The company are in high spirits, but exhausted. Since I saw them last, they've teched, dressed, previewed and opened Greg's production of *The Island Princess*.

In today's Evening Standard there's an interview with me, headlined 'The RSC Made A Mistake' – my views on Project Fleet. Greg reports that the RSC hierarchy are angry with me: *Just when we'd turned a corner!* Are they crazy? Has everyone developed amnesia? Or gone into denial? Project Fleet brought the RSC to the brink of destruction. We're still only inches away from the edge. As demonstrated by the ludicrous struggle to bring this hit season to London, and now to find an audience here. Theatre history will judge Adrian very harshly I think – and I say that with regret because he's a tremendous director – but in the meantime he's just been given a big golden handshake with a series of farewell parties, toasts and gifts. The polite Englishness of it is bizarre to me.

And I'm not allowed to talk about this?! Me, who's worked for this company for twenty-one years – a lot longer than some of the present hierarchy – and served it well. This is *my* RSC too. And – what – I mustn't talk about it?! Where are we? Apartheid South Africa? Nazi Germany?

Friday 13th December 2002

Today's date lived up its reputation. First preview of *Roman Actor,* and unfortunately The Fear descended badly. Began with a few minor stumbles on some lines. Survived each effortlessly at the time, but then there's always the aftershock. This led to the babbling voices . . . one of them started testing out lines that were coming up . . . another said don't risk it, leave it to the moment . . . another saying I can't take this. Inbetween scenes, I had to go into backstage corners, grimacing, flicking my head, tring to disperse the racket in my head. Sometimes I caught myself inadvertently doing this onstage. In the interval I dashed up to the dressing room, grabbed the script, and went through the lines of the second half. I'd already gone over all the lines of the play four times today!

Afterwards, to my surprise, Sean (Holmes, director) said it was a good show. Luckily I'm playing a fiercely paranoid character, the Emperor Domitian, so his demons and mine feed off one another greedily. But Jesus it's weird. The way that The Fear descends, terrorises, and goes. The show finishes, life comes back to normal. And then I start work the next night knowing I've probably got an appointment with The Fear again. It's almost routine now. It's like the normal fear of going onstage, the kind all actors experience, and live with, and barely notice – it's like that, but gone haywire.

The good news is that there were 500 people in the audience. The bad news is that 300 of these were comps. Thelma and Bill are comping these early performances heavily. A decent sized house cheers everyone up – cast and audience – it creates an illusion of success, which can then (hopefully) transform into the real thing.

But I remain puzzled as to why the RSC's London audience isn't automatically flocking to the Gielgud as they would've done to the Barbican. In the old days, when popular shows transferred from Stratford, they'd sell out straightaway. Where is our audience? Is their absence a form of punishment for Project Fleet? Are they still angry with us? Stupid question. *I'm* still angry with us.

Saturday 14th December 2002

The press performance of *Roman Actor* went well. The house was big and friendly, and The Fear took a night off, thank God, and just allowed me to get on with it. This was important because I think Domitian is one of the best things I've done, and I wanted to serve it up decently.

Tomorrow we fly off for a fortnight in South Africa and Namibia, while the last two Jacobethans – *Edward III* and *Eastward Ho!* – open at the Gielgud.

During these frantically busy days, I managed one brief conversation with Mic:

'Any news from Turin?'

'Not a word.'

'Any hope before Christmas?'

'Possibly not . . . I don't honestly know.'

'Anything more we should be doing?'

'I don't think there is. We must just – '

' – Be patient.'

'Exactly. Have a good holiday. Give the sunshine my love.'

Mic is a real fighter, but I could hear a tone of resignation in her voice. Everyone seems to be sending out the same signal: this ain't gonna work.

Friday 20th December 2002

Cape Grace Hotel, Waterfront, Cape Town. The first week has produced mixed emotions. I'm prejudiced of course, but Cape Town is the most beautiful city in the world, with the most beautiful mountain, and the most beautiful blue sky, and the most beautiful deep sea, which stretches south from here to the end of the world.

Mom met us at the airport. In the same way that children can shoot up if you don't see them for a while, old people can shrink, deflate, and in a way vanish. The last time we embraced (when Greg and I were leaving at the end of our 2001 trip), Mom suddenly said, 'I don't think we're going to see one another again.' I laughed and said, 'Oh nonsense', but to some extent it's come true, because the person I'm with this time is not altogether familiar. She, who followed my career almost obsessively, is now confused by my shaved head – for Domitian. She has no awareness that I'm currently doing any shows.

You quickly learn to avoid asking questions. She's fine, almost normal, provided she just has to comment and react. So we've been telling her lots of stories about our summer in Stratford this year. She enjoys these hugely – her laugh is just the same – and then forgets them instantly. Oddly enough, the illness – it's now diagnosed as Alzheimer's, as the family warned – is making her gentler, more affectionate, more tactile. The all-knowing, all-controlling Jewish Mother, the formidable Matriach, has gone forever. And just in one year . . . ! There's an uncensored side now. She keeps saying, 'I can't believe you're here, I'm so thrilled, so thrilled,' in a tone of almost childish wonder. And there was a funny moment over lunch the other day in Camps Bay's fish restaurant, Blues. She was talking about Dad, and how she misses him more and more. This came as a surprise to me; they weren't natural soul-mates, and had a combative relationship. Forgetting my rule about not asking questions, I said, 'When d'you think you were happiest?' She looked blank for a moment, then answered, 'In bed.' Greg, who was about to pop a prawn in his mouth, froze in astonishment. Blushing, I said,'What?' She said, 'Yes, he was very good in bed.' Greg's prawn flew across the room.

So, as I say, a week of mixed emotions.

Topped by this fax, which has just arrived from Mic:

Alas, Carmen Zuilli from Einaudi writes: 'I'm sorry for the delay on my answer, but I've just heard from the Primo Levi Estate. I'm afraid they don't give permission for a performance from Levi's *If This Is A Man*. The Levi Estate and our publishing house thank Sir Antony Sher for the undoubted seriousness of the proposal.'

'They don't give permission for a performance from Levi's *If This Is A Man*.' That sounds pretty final. And all-encompassing. As if they just automatically turn down all requests. Which is probably the case. Someone – who was it? – told us that they simply don't let anyone near this particular book. And even though I'm hurting at the moment, I still respect them for it.

But I just don't believe they've considered my proposal carefully enough. I'm asking permission to do the most faithful, untheatrical rendition of Levi's book. Which would bring his writing to a whole new audience. How on earth can that be a bad thing?

I suddenly feel such a stupid idiot. For writing it – without first getting the rights – and for all those ridiculous discussions about how to do it, where to do it, etc. And meanwhile the Estate just routinely refuse all callers. Jesus.

What do I do?

Do I abandon *Primo*, and ask to see the stage version of *If This Is A Man* which Primo Levi co-wrote in the '60's? The one which got panned. And which would require me and other actors to shave our heads, and don striped uniforms, artfully dirtied.

I think not.

Right – so is there anything more to be done?

Mom – not the Mom now, but the one before, the Jewish Mother, the Matriach – she would have said don't take no for an answer, find a way round this.

But – sorry to ask a question, Mom – what might that be?

Part Two

Not Doing Primo

Sunday 29th December 2002

It's a very cruel experience to fly into London at 6.30 am in the middle of winter after two weeks in Africa. This morning was the darkest, wettest, coldest day in creation. By the time the taxi reached Islington, the sky was finally lightening (oh, think of the dawns we've seen recently) and releasing that peculiar ghostly blue of December mornings in England. We'd forgotten to set the central heating properly, so the house was freezing, and we spent the first couple of hours wandering around in our outdoor coats.

Worst of all was me having to go through my *Malcontent* lines. Unbelievably, I'm back on stage tomorrow night. I'm not sure I even *like* acting anymore.

Monday 13th January 2003

Plan to do some painting again. After the disappointment of what happened to *Primo* – or didn't happen – I have no appetite for writing, and need to find something else to fill each day before going in to work at the Gielgud. A painting of a giant wave is waiting to be started, but that's too intimidating to contemplate yet, so I'll warm up by tinkering with some of the existing ones. There's easy work to be done on both the *Macbeth* picture (Harriet Walter and self, naked, bloody, howling, in a vice-like embrace), and the portrait of Mom which she sat for when she was here in '99. The latter is stacked with other canvases in my painting cupboard. As I touch it I know something's wrong. A stickiness. Turns out to be mould: furry patches everywhere, ugly little black rivulets. I now discover that the extractor pipe which goes through the cupboard – from the drying machine in the next room – is slightly split. It's been pumping damp air among the paintings for God knows how long. I take them all out, but none is ruined as badly as the one of Mom. Given her illness, this is unbearable. I try cleaning it, but only make it worse. Most of the mould comes off, but so does a lot of oil paint, especially from the dark areas, don't know why. So now I'm left with a portrait of a ghost. In despair, I grab a pair of scissors and start hacking up the whole thing. Greg stops me as I reach the head – luckily – and we find we can salvage a striking image of her face caught among a haze of light clouds and sworls, which is actually residue from the damage. But if I'd set out to paint a portrait of someone with Alzheimers, I could never have achieved this. It's quite haunting. I must dry it out properly, and think about framing it . . .

Tuesday 14th January 2003

Mic rings. Our conversations about *Primo* have become half-hearted I'm afraid. Shall we try this, shall we try that? Today's news is that she's having difficulty tracking down the film director whom Paul Bailey said might help, Francesco Rosi. Turns out he knew Primo Levi personally, and that's how he got permission from the family to film *The Truce* even after its author died. I don't think this is going to lead anywhere.

Wednesday 15th January 2003

Thelma rings to secretly impart the news that Greg is being given the Olivier Award for Outstanding Achievement for the Jacobethan Season. I ring the Clapham rehearsal rooms, get him dragged out of his *Taming of the Shrew* rehearsal, and tell him. He sounds wonderfully flabbergasted. We've already been rewarded with a tremendous increase in the bookings – we now play to packed houses – and this is the cherry on the cake.

I lunch with Richard before he flies off to Australia for a holiday. Like when I rang him from Cape Town, he's still completely unfazed by our rejection from the Primo Levi Estate. He's sure we can apply again if we can just get some heavyweight backing next time; ie. a theatre that wants to produce it. In fact, while I was away he showed the script to Ian Rickson at the Royal Court, on the strict understanding that we didn't have the rights and a script shouldn't even exist yet. Rickson was impressed by it, but didn't feel it was a Court play, wasn't even sure it qualified as new writing. So where next? Our best chance, the RSC, is out of the picture unfortunately; Project Fleet erased both its venues for new plays, The Other Place and The Pit. At the National, its smallest auditorium, the Cottesloe, is perfect, but when I met Nick Hytner he didn't sound like he wanted to do this kind of thing. I offer to ring him anyway. Nothing to be lost. Richard now launches into a discussion about how we'd rehearse it. (It's exciting talking like this again, though dangerous.) Richard feels we might start with a workshop, which might involve other actors. Says that to even remotely touch Levi's experience in the camp, we need to do some exercises which involve humiliation. Humiliation improvisations maybe, situations of humiliation. He keeps saying this word, 'humiliation'. Since Richard is my sternest critic (I have to brace myself whenever he comes to my shows), I eventually interrupt and say, 'But Richard why would I need humiliation exercises when I've asked *you* to direct?'

Afterwards, I wonder how serious he was. And what exactly would 'humiliation' entail?

Back at home, I ring the National and manage to get straight through to Nick. I'm completely honest about the situation. He promises to read the script. Sounds guarded, but says in principle there's no reason why a one-man show couldn't be in the Cottesloe.

Monday 20th January 2003

A dark rainy day, the mother of all Mondays. In the evening we go to Portcullis House, next to Westminister, to a special preview screening of *The Pianist* arranged by Lord Janner, Chairman of the Holocaust Educational Trust. As we arrive, I bump into a bearded, burly figure wearing a yamulka. 'Ah,' we say to one another: 'We went to Auschwitz together.' He's the rabbi – another South African – who conducted the tour of the camp when I visited in 2001, along with Ian McKellen. These tours are run by the Trust for school parties – pupils and teachers – and are both brilliant and bizarre. They're done in one day: you do a 'day trip' to Auschwitz. Early in the morning you fly from Luton to Krakóv, you're driven by coach to Auschwitz, you're guided round the two existing camps, then it's back to Krakóv, back to Luton, and this sad and shocking day ends with you tucked up in your own bed again.

The Pianist is excellent. The detail of life in the ghetto feels authentic – Polanski experienced it first-hand as a child – and he has the good sense to never try showing the camps. Cousin Ronnie has done a terrific screenplay, allowing the story to be told in odd fragments and episodes. You sense the grim weight of the war all around you, yet only glimpse it, in the same way that the main character does: peering through the windows of his different hiding places.

While we watched the film, Ronnie and wife Natasha went to *Island Princess* at the Gielgud, and then we all met up for supper. Much laughter, as always. Although Ronnie and I have both been in this country for decades, we weren't close, we seldom saw one another. Then in 2001 Greg and I did *Mahler's Conversion*, Ronnie's fine play about the composer/conductor. It was savaged by the critics; one of those times when they seem to operate like a pack of African wild dogs, expertly working together to bring down their prey, eating on the run. We had to close. It was a distressing and unjust experience, but it brought us and the Harwoods very close, and that's been heart-warming. So some good came out of it.

Saturday 15th February 2003

Day of the Peace March to try and stop the Iraq war. We had two performances of *Malcontent*. The West End was eerily quiet when I arrived at about noon, with roads cordoned off, and police vans parked everywhere. But just after I finished lunch, I saw the march arrive in Shaftesbury Avenue. Actually I heard them before I saw them – it's the same noise as when you pass a football stadium: a phenomenal volume of people – and then they spilled into view, like floodwater down a dry river bed, and kept coming. Although this was a march for peace, any mass demo carries such power there's a feeling of violence in the air. Dom's modern-dress production of *Malcontent* has a soundscape of huge crowds, helicopters and hooters. During the matinee, it was impossible to distinguish this from the real thing outside. When we finished, the march was *still* passing. An astonishing turn-out. It might actually make a difference, halt this madness. Things used to be simpler. The Second World War, Primo Levi's war, was a clear case of good versus evil.

Primo is back in my thoughts because Nick Hytner likes the script, and yes we could do it in the Cottesloe, possibly in autumn next year, *if* we can sort out the rights. Nick has asked the NT's Literary Manager, Jack Bradley, to look into it. Jack and Mic are in conversation. I'm trying to be very laid back, trying not to even think about it . . .

Friday 7th March 2003

From the sublime to the ridiculous. While a question mark still hangs over whether I'll be allowed to play someone who survived the Holocaust, I've now been asked to play the man who unleashed it. Hitler. It's a film, a dark satiric comedy called *Churchill: The Hollywood Years*, written and to be directed by Peter Richardson. In the story, Churchill is portrayed as a hunky GI (Christian Slater), since the war couldn't have possibly been won by a fat old Englishman. Hitler and Eva Braun (Miranda Richardson) are brought over to Buckingham Palace by a corrupt British aristo (Leslie Philips) to broker a deal with George V (Harry Enfield) and his pretty young heir Princess Elizabeth (Neve Campbell).

Spent this morning watching some of the Hitler documentaries I collected when I played him before, in *Arturo Ui*. As in that play, and as in Chaplin's *The Great Dictator*, the Hitler in our film is a clown. But I neverthelss feel strangely excited by the prospect of crawling into the skin of the Beast again. Will I get into trouble for it though? The other day, at another Holocaust Educational Trust event, Greville Janner asked what I was doing after the Jacobethans. Without thinking, I said, 'Playing Hitler in a film.' He went white. I quickly added, 'It's alright, it's a comedy.' He went whiter.

Well sorry, but like some of my heroes – Shakespeare and the Jacobethans for starters – I'm drawn to seeking laughs in hell.

A meeting about *Primo* with Jack Bradley and Mic. Ironically, we had to gather at the Royal Court because Richard is working there and could only spare his lunch break. We bumped into Max Stafford-Clark, and you could see him trying to work out the mathematics:

Richard (Court) + Tony (RSC) + Jack (National) = ?

Jack was very gung ho, determined to find a way of winning round the family, saying that as a last resort he'd fly to Turin himself, and doorstep Levi's widow outside their home. In the meantime, he and Nick H. will draft a letter, expressing the National's passionate interest in the project, and then have this translated into Italian, so that the family can read it for themselves. Until we communicate with them directly, we can never be quite sure how we're being represented.

Sunday 9th March 2003

Exhausted. My two shows have been over-scheduled in the extension at the Gielgud: the powers-that-be hoped my name might bring in the punters. Wrong. The whole experience has been entirely unpredictable. After a slow start, our first six-week run played to capacity, whichever show was on, but then as soon as we extended, despite great reviews, great word-of-mouth, and Greg's Olivier Award, the audiences vanished again. We now play to about 200 per performance, virtually unchanging, and again irrespective of which show is on. A mystery. The only good news is that there's been a diminishing of The Fear with these smaller audiences. Does that mean The Fear relates to Success?

Meanwhile, last week we heard that Richard E. Grant is out of the running as Verwoerd in *I.D.* The favourite now seems to be the renowned Fugard veteran, the South African actor Marius Weyers. Let's hope he likes the script.

In my weekly phone call to Mom this evening, she said, as she now says regularly, the same two things: 'Oh how lovely to hear your voice!' and 'So – still no work?' The latter is a puzzle. I guess the precise moment when the illness took hold must have coincided with that awful period of unemployment I had in 2001. So that's stuck in her mind now. She thinks she's the mother of an out-of-work-actor. I imagine her telling people: 'Antony went overseas to try his luck as an actor, but it's very

difficult there, and, shame, it just never worked out for him.'
She who was so ambitious for me, she who revelled in whatever
I achieved, she now laments my failure. It makes Greg and me
laugh. She's still the archetypal Jewish Mother, whose son is
just a big disappointment.

Tuesday 18th March 2003

Yesterday, on a beautiful spring day, President Bush gave
Saddam Hussein this ultimatum: go into exile in the next 48
hours or we're coming in to get you. Dear God help us all.

But no He won't actually. In fact He's the problem. We now
have two fundamentalist religious states squaring up to one
another. The question is how did we, Britain, get involved in
this?

As the deadline ticks away today, it makes my own trials and
tribulations seem unimportant. Nevertheless, an event this
afternoon could make or break *Primo*. Months ago, Ronnie's
Italian translator reported there was a chap at Einaudi, Roberto
Gilodi, who was fluent in English, and might be helpful. At the
time we didn't get in touch because we were dealing with
someone else. But now, as the National throw everything
they've got into securing the rights, Gilodi has become the new
contact, our man in Turin. And he happens to be here at the
moment, visiting the London Book Fair. So Jack and Mic are
having a meeting with him at the National at teatime. Unfortunately, I've got two *Roman Actors* today, so I can't make it. But
this is our best chance yet. For the first time we're going to be
talking to a person and not an Estate.

After the matinee I tried ringing Mic's mobile, but it was on
answerphone-mode. Maybe the meeting was still going on, and
maybe that was a good sign. It was agony not to know.

The evening show was no ordinary one. A royal visit. Because
of the war, it's been on-off over the last few days, but in the end
Prince Charles and Camilla Parker-Bowles arrived at the

Gielgud. The performance turned into a hall of mirrors. During the various plays-within-the-play sequences, there was an actor playing royalty (me) watching actors playing actors, while real royalty (Charles) watched us all.

There's always a rather tense moment in the interval of a royal visit, when word comes round whether they want to meet the cast or not. It's the thumbs-up or thumbs-down from Caesar. It was thumbs-up tonight, and at the end when they came onstage behind the curtain it was clear they'd enjoyed it hugely.

Then I dashed home and got hold of Mic at last. She said the meeting with Gilodi had gone extremely well. Apparently it was a masterstroke by Jack to hold it at the National. Gilodi was more than impressed. He made several (cautiously) encouraging remarks. He will now report back to the family, and the National will send our letter – translated into Italian – for them to read.

Mic said, 'I think we're in with a chance.'

Monday 24th March 2003

Devon. Filming *Churchill*. I came straight down here after the Jacobethans finished on Saturday, and shot my first scene yesterday. It was quite intimidating, since the room was chock-ablock with top British comedy stars – H. Enfield, L. Philips, Reeves and Mortimer, Phil Cornwall – and then me. I decided to play it dead straight, which was probably wise.

This morning, as a group of us were driven to location through beautiful countryside in soft dawn light, we listened to the news from Iraq on the *Today* programme. The war there is possibly more surreal than the one we're filming here. Saddam has about half a dozen doubles (the resemblances are impressive, even better than my Hitler make-up, which is pretty good) so even if the coalition troops catch him, they might never know if it's the right one.

It was the Oscar ceremony in Los Angeles last night. I was standing to the side of the set today, watching the others at work, when the producer, Jonathan Cavendish, whispered to me that he'd just heard the results, and that Ronnie had won Best Screenplay for *The Pianist*. I let out such a yelp of joy it ruined the take. An Oscar for Ronnie: there's justice, after what happened to *Mahler*.

Thursday 27th March 2003

Ralph Richardson said that stage acting is the art of keeping a large group of people from coughing. I'd like to mention that film acting is the art of keeping yourself from going completely fucking nuts with boredom.

Today, my pick-up time at the hotel was 6.30 am, and I got back at 9.30 pm, fifteen hours later, having spent thirteen hours waiting, with only two on set. And I never got to say my one line of dialogue!

This is not a job for workaholics.

And of course once you're made-up and costumed as Hitler, your freedom of movement becomes rather restricted. During your hours off, there's no popping into the local Waterstone's. I sometimes wander round the unit base, but since this is on a large car park, I encounter members of the public, and get upset when they giggle and give the Sieg Heil salute. I know it makes no sense, but while I'm dressed like this I'll do the gags round here, thank you.

So then I confine myself to my trailer, which is the size of a horsebox. This is a low-budget movie, and only the two American stars get proper Winnebagos. I always bring books to read and sketchbooks to fill, but a weird apathy takes over, and I end up on the little bed, drifting in and out of dull, sluggish sleep. This afternoon I was out for about two hours! Waking, I had no idea where I was. I struggled off the bed, and suddenly found myself face to face with Hitler. I screamed out loud. For a Jew to wake from sleep, look in a mirror, and see Hitler looking back is a shock of existential proportions.

At least I had a soulmate today: the actor David Schneider playing Goebbels. When we met we said almost in unison, 'What are two nice Jewish guys doing in a job like this?' We walked together to the set, turned a corner and both stopped dead. In front of us were thirty uniformed Stormtroopers – the young local extras carefully selected for their chiselled, blonde, Aryan looks.

David said in a hushed voice, 'As a little boy I had nightmares like this.'

I sighed; 'As a big boy I've had fantasies like this.'

Saturday / Sunday 7th / 8th June 2003

With filming on *Churchill* over, I'm able to join the Doran family reunion in Stratford. Ma and Pa Doran are staying with us at the Welcombe Hotel, and the rest are at the Moat House: Greg's older brother Mark and family, his older sister Jo, and also his twin Ruth, who's over from America, where she lives, also married to a Tony. He's not been able to come, but their two small boys are here, Evan and little Greg. It's very charming the way they call us 'Uncle Greg, Uncle Tony' in their American accents. On Saturday afternoon, some of the adults went to the matinee of big Greg's production of *The Taming of the Shrew* (the critics have enthused about this as much as I did), while we took the kids rowing on the Avon with Jo. Great hilarity. The kids were much better at it than we were.

On Sunday, the papers carried articles about gay partnerships being recognised by law. If this goes through parliament, it'll be tremendous news. Aside from tax and property rights, the most important thing is next-of-kin status. There are appalling stories of one partner being injured and unconscious, and the other forbidden access by the family. Even though this wouldn't be the case with us, it's vital to fight for this law.

Over lunch with the Doran clan, we discussed how we'd finally do the celebration, a mere sixteen years after our relationship began: a small official service followed by a big party. It always moves me that Greg's parents, John and Margaret, who are devout Catholics, seem totally comfortable with conversations like this. Among much laughter, we even put in requests for our trousseau. Knowing my tastes, Mark offered to get us a big *braai* (Afrikaans for barbecue).

Sunday 29th June 2003

I feel I've been run over by a truck. (Mind you, when people say that, how do they know?) It's the end of my first week on another film: *Home*, a sixty-minute BBC4 adaptation of J.G. Ballard's short story, *The Enormous Space*. Couldn't be more different from *Churchill*. I've not spent a single second sitting round waiting, since it's virtually a one-man show on camera; I'm alone for about 80% of the action. I play a man who decides to shut his front door on the world, and to survive solely on the resources within his own house. When the food stocks run out, he starts to trap neighbours' pets, and then things get even worse. It's a classic Ballardian tale of suburban madness, shocking and funny, and right up my street. And my input is being encouraged by both the director/writer Richard Curson-Smith (who did that sly and hilarious BBC4 film about Dali, *Surrealissimo*) and the producer Richard Fell (who runs the Fiction Lab department). I've been researching, improvising with the other actors, and working with Richard C-S on rewrites of the script. Freed from the committees and the caution of mainstream TV, Fiction Lab is able to function more like fringe theatre. There's not much money, but if you all muck in you can make magic. I'm relishing it. In fact, it's the best TV/film experience of my career. And it's already earned me one of my best reviews. When Richard C-S wrote to J.G. Ballard about the project he replied immediately, endorsing everything, and saying about me: 'He's an actor that can go mad in the blink of an eye.' I'm thinking of printing this quote next to my photo in the actors' directory, *Spotlight*.

If only the Primo Levi Estate would show the same enthusiasm, but I'm afraid Turin has gone very quiet again.

Thursday 10th July 2003

Masseria San Domenico, province of Apulia, heel of Italy. We're on holiday here for two weeks, with me trying to recover from *Home*, and get ready for *I.D.* This hotel was originally a 15th-century fortress: giant blocks of white stone against bright blue skies.

At 5.30pm today Mic rings through with incredible news. They've said yes. The Primo Levi Estate has said yes. Nine months since I tried that first draft, seven months since their initial rejection, and three months since Roberto Gilodi's visit to London, they've said yes. Their only condition is that I write the script as simply and faithfully as in the proposal. They don't know that I already have. Good God. We could do this next autumn, straight after the RSC *Othello* which Greg and I are planning. That is, if Nick H. has kept open a slot for us in the Cottesloe. I ask Mic to ring and thank Jack Bradley at the NT – he's been heroic on this – and to let Paul Lyon-Maris know as well; I'll need representation as an actor as well (I have to get used to this idea). Then I ring Richard, and although I only get his answerphone, I send a whoop of joy across Europe.

Is it significant that this has happened while we're here in Italy? Probably not, but after Mic's call we go for a walk – actually, it's more a dance – and when we're beside the olive grove, a little bird, a local bird, one we can't identify, keeps flitting round and landing near us. Greg says, 'Look, there he is – there's Primo – say thank you.'

During our stay here, I have the most unusual and enjoyable task ever in preparation for a role. I have to get fat. (Tsafendas

had a giant tapeworm, or imagined he did, and was always
eating for two.) Imagine coming on holiday to Italy, and being
told you *have* to put on weight. I've been embracing the chal-
lenge with commitment. I'm currently at 12 stone 10 lbs, and
hope to get to 13 and a half, the heaviest I've ever been. Every
meal consists of bread, pasta and red wine. Also, we're having
a very stationary holiday, sprawled alongside the pool. Luckily,
I've struck gold with my first book – *The Life of Pi* – I can't put
it down. They say there are only about half a dozen stories in
the world, and that all books and plays are simply variations on
them. Well, I think Yann Martell has just invented a new one.
It's so full of beauty and wonder I can't see straight.

Mind you, it could also be the sheer intake of alcohol on this
particular evening. When we go to bed, I keep crashing into
things. 'Why am I so pissed?' I ask.

'It's relief,' Greg says gently; 'You can do *Primo*. You've been
holding your breath for a long time.'

20th July–18th October 2003. During these three months I do I.D.
*at the Almeida. Since this is a story in itself, I'll just represent it
symbolically, by selecting one key day:*

Thursday 28th August 2003

Woke in the early hours gripped with such panic I thought my
chest would burst. I knew I had to turn a corner. Just as pure
survival. I would collapse otherwise. I would be ill.

(Of course a part of me wants to be ill, wants to be let off,
excused from duty – like at school – sent home, put to bed.)

Got up, came down to my study, and wrote this:

Later today is the first ever performance of my first ever
play. (The first preview of *I.D.*) I must embrace this. No,
celebrate it. My play is being done, and done well, I think.

Despite all the frights and problems along the way, I must give it a chance now. And give my performance as Tsafendas a chance too. There's still plenty of time to get things right, to correct the little things driving me mad. Like the dot-matrix on the back of the set, which keeps flashing up info. about places and dates, and makes you feel you're watching a foreign film, and won't be able to follow it if you don't read the subtitles. Outsiders will come to the previews, and reassure Nancy (Meckler, director) and Katrina (Lindsay, designer) that their work is good enough without this semaphore. I must save my strength for myself now. I must use everything that's happened – the difficulties I've had doing rewrites while playing the main part, the difficulties some of the other actors have had finding their characters – I must use everything that's left me feeling battered, exhausted and dislocated: I must use it because it corresponds exactly to the circumstances of Tsafendas' own life. The worst times as an actor are when you have to play a calm and controlled character while you yourself are feeling shaky inside. But in this case, I can carry all the crap in the world onstage with me.

Went back to bed, fell asleep, and woke feeling a lot calmer, better than I've been in ages. It's amazing – it's just about mental will. Had a good laugh with Greg. Told him that as I was leaving the Almeida bar last night I said to the others: 'Well, this time tomorrow I'll have lost my virginity as a playwright', and Jon Cartwright (playing Gavronsky) immediately piped up: 'Oh I'm thinking of this week more as foreplay – it's not till press night we'll get full penetration.'

Back at the theatre this morning, we carried on with the tech, then did a dress rehearsal in the afternoon. Several big problems occured in the second half, most worryingly when the ropes didn't descend for for the prison cell/cage. There was a brief discussion about cancelling tonight's performance, but we decided to proceed. If we have to stop we'll stop. It's only a preview, after all.

The evening was upon us in a flash. I paced round my dressing room, catching glimpses of myself in the mirror and feeling pleased. Tsafendas was there. My feasting in Italy resulted in a good bear-like shape (I got up to 13 stone 4lbs), and the cosmetic tan has produced a convincingly ambiguous skin colour to represent Tsafendas' mixed-race identity. The costume's good too: shabby, stained, creased, the pockets weighed down with years of miniature trash, the little straw hat smashed out of shape. I tried the voice – deep, hoarse, wrecked also – and it felt right. Even if I wasn't completely sure about the play yet, the performance seemed ready.

There was a knock on the door, and Jenny Woodburne (playing Betsie Verwoerd) looked in and said the cast were having a final get-together onstage and would I like to join them? Of course! We stood in a circle and sang NKosi Sikelel' Afrika. I could hardly join in. Big sobs threatened to come up. This of all songs. With this group of good people.

Emotion almost overcame me again as the show began, and I spoke Tsafendas' first line: 'I dream of a girl waiting for me somewhere in Africa . . . ' Then I got a grip of myself, and everything became more dream-like. The house was full, but a bit quiet. Marius Weyers (Verwoerd) had a stumble in his first big oration – which stopped my heart, sitting onstage, my back to the audience – but he also got some laughs, which will give him more confidence with the speech. I got laughs throughout the evening too, and the audience clearly enjoyed the electricity generated by Alex Ferns (Lintwurm, the tapeworm). But generally the play didn't work satirically quite as I hoped. It seemed to shock and move people more than amuse them. I think. Who knows? It was a weird, blurred experience. At the curtain call, we took one bow as planned, but they kept clapping, so we went back.

Alone in the dressing room, I felt an overwhelming sense of flatness. And strange anger. That was it – the first performance of my first play – and I somehow missed it.

Mike Attenborough came in. After being initially supportive, tremendously so, championing the play, Mike has cooled recently, and I'm not sure why. He seems to communicate anxiety now. Maybe it's because he's announced that his new regime at the Almeida is mainly about new works, and I'm the first one in. Tonight he said he was very worried about Act One, and we needed to have a big talk. I said I couldn't really put on the writer's hat at the moment. The show was so technically demanding in terms of its choreography, its entrances and exits, its props and its costume canges, that I needed to have one more preview to learn it all, just as an actor. So I proposed that we have our post-mortem after tomorrow's show – Friday. Then if there were rewrites – which there will be – I'd do them on Saturday, hand them out after the show, so the actors could learn them on Sunday, and then we'd put them in on Monday. Mike agreed to this schedule, but left looking unhappy.

Nancy came in next. She's also been very jumpy during rehearsals, very suspicious of the script, despite nurturing it from its earliest conception – *what is it about new plays?* – but now at last, thank God, she just radiated pride and happiness. Said she'd found Tsafendas himself very moving tonight.

And finally Greg, full of emotion and praise. As he hugged me, I caught sight of myself in the mirror. I looked blank.

Out in the foyer, people were very buzzy, very enthused by the evening. I couldn't get my bearings: *the audience is excited, the producer is worried, the director is both excited and worried, the leading actor is pleased, the writer is in shock . . .*

As we walked home – and it's handy living round the corner from work – Greg suddenly stopped me and said, 'Look I need you to hear this, and hear it clearly. You're telling an extraordinary story about an extraordinary man, a man who's slipped from view, slipped away, slipped into one of the cracks of history. But now you're telling his story. And that's really worthwhile!'

Monday 6th October 2003

'I'll never do it again,' I said to Richard yesterday; 'I'll never again play the main part in a play I've written.'

'*Primo* is different,' he argued; 'It's not really your play. It's just Primo Levi's words. And we can get these right, get the script right, before we even go into rehearsal.'

'No,' I said; 'Now can we please talk about Henry Goo – '

'No we can't,' he said; 'If you don't act it, I'm not directing it. It's as simple as that.'

So here we are now, travelling up in the lift to Nick Hytner's office at the National. Despite the struggle to secure *Primo* as a project, and despite the success of *I.D.* – we got great reviews and are playing to full houses – I feel shaken by the Almeida experience, and don't want it again. But it seems to be happening all the same. I feel that I keep proceeding into unsafe places. This is a Geminian thing. On the one hand you don't want something, on the other hand you do.

We thought we were going to be sumptuously lunched and schmoozed by Nick, but in typically austere fashion it's sandwiches and fruit juice in his office. More of a surprise is the fact that he doesn't really have an autumn space for us next year, so what about spring 2005? I said no straightaway: it's too long to wait, and now that we've got the green light, let's just go. Richard agreed. Nick said he'd look at his schedules again. We left feeling unsettled, but I suppose the Cottesloe slots are the ones everyone grabs first. When people criticise the Barbican, they forget to mention that although the surrounding concrete environment is gruesome, at least it has a superb main auditorium. Which can't be said of the Olivier or the Lyttelton. The Cottesloe is the National's only intrinsically good space.

Tonight, while I was onstage in *I.D.* , the BBC4 film of *Home* was screened. The preview notices have been terrific. The Times said it was one of the best TV dramas of the year.

So this is a time to celebrate. Greg and I have also finally secured – after two years of hounding and begging – a commercial video and DVD of our Channel 4 *Macbeth* film. We feel very proud of this: a permanent record of what's probably our best ever collaboration.

Wednesday 22nd October 2003

My sister Verne and her partner Joan flew over for the final night of *I.D.* last weekend, and today I took them to the Tate Modern, to see Olafur Eliasson's *Weather Project*. A colossal installation in the entrance hall, it consists of a gently glowing sun on the far wall, a light yellowish mist permeating the area, and, most wonderfully, a mirror covering the high ceiling. So everything is reflected and doubled, including us visitors. We're like little ants up there, waving at ourselves to try and locate who's who. Or else we lie on the floor and gaze up at what now looks like a flight of angels in space. The whole thing creates a sense of peace and wonder, and makes everyone smile.

As promised, Nick H. has revised his schedule and come up with a new proposal. We could do a very short run of *Primo* in autumn 2004 – no more than a dozen performances – then have a long gap, during which I'll either tour it or do another show at the National, and then play it again in spring 2005.

The biggest problem is that the start date of the workshop which Richard wants to do (at the beginning of August) definitely limits the life of the RSC *Othello*. This is shaping up excitingly. Playing the man himself will be my fellow South African, Sello Maake ka Ncube, who played Shakespeare's other great black role, Aaron, when Greg and I did *Titus Andronicus* in South Africa in 1995. For *Othello* there's talk of all sorts of possibilities – a Japanese tour, a London run (if the RSC can

find a bloody theatre again), a Channel 4 film like *Macbeth*. But
if all of these things were to happen, there probably isn't
enough time now – before the *Primo* workshop. How to break
the news to Greg? He already sees my move to the National as
a slight betrayal. He's full of excitement about being in rehearsal with Judi Dench for *All's Well That Ends Well*, and I don't
want to spoil it for him. Yet every time we're alone together I
feel a peculiar sense of guilt. It's like I'm having an affair.

Monday 25th November 2003

A special day's filming on the TV series, *Murphy's Law*. I'm
playing a coke-crazed theatre actor who specialises in psycho-
paths – *hey, how did they come to cast me?* – and who may or may
not be a modern-day Jack the Ripper. Today we did the scenes
in his dressing room, when he chops and snorts coke. All very
familiar. Except for the film crew surrounding me. The props
guy asked what I wanted to use for the coke. The choice was
baby powder or glucose. Both sounded disgusting. I was half
inclined to say, 'Oh just pop out and score me a gram of the
real thing', but didn't of course. I chose glucose. It tasted like
nothing.

Later got into conversation with the star of the series,
Jimmy Nesbitt, who's immensely charming. He said he'd had
a very, very late night. He went to the premiere of an Irish film,
and they had had 'a wee bit of an Irish party.' This was told
with a twinkle in his dark eye. I suppose it's similar to my own
perennial excuse for myself: I'm a gay Jewish white South
African, what d'you expect?

Sunday 30th November 2003

Stratford. We're back. It's beautiful. This morning we got up
to a great view through the big front window of our Avonside
flat. From a cloudless sky the low winter sun hit the river with

such an explosion of brightness you had to shade your eyes. The water threw a play of light onto the white walls of the room. The bells of Trinity Church began to ring out, and if we were believers we would've knelt down and given thanks. Instead we just sat there, dazed with pleasure.

Greg's here to open *All's Well*, and I've got two tasks: to learn Iago, and to do a new draft of *Primo*. This will be submitted to the Levi Estate, who have script approval. The National have scheduled some extra performances next autumn – we're now up to about 20 – and I've told Greg about the start date; he wasn't overjoyed, but will get over it.

I immediately establish my daily routine here: learn lines from 8 – 11, write till lunch and after.

The first task with *Primo* is to remove the new ending I wrote: the return journey to Italy, and the transformation of an atom of carbon into a dot on a page, like the transformation of the experience of Auschwitz into a major book. It's wrong. The story needs to end simply with the liberation of the camp, when the Russians arrive on the 27th January 1945. Trouble is, Levi mentions this only very briefly as he finishes *If This Is A Man*, in just one sentence: 'The Russians arrived while Charles and I were carrying Sómogyi a little distance outside.' He then describes it with much more detail and eloquence at the beginning of *The Truce*: 'Four young soldiers on horseback . . . four men, armed, but not against us: four messengers of peace . . . ' The passage continues with his remarkable section on the shame which overwhelms the liberators as they stare at the inmates: 'It was that shame we knew so well, the shame that drowned us after the selections, and every time we had to watch, or submit to, some outrage: the shame . . . that the just man experiences at another man's crime; the feeling of guilt that such a crime should exist.' This would make a perfect coda to my piece, but will the Estate allow me to borrow a few lines from *The Truce*?

Evening. Dirty Duck. A welcome party for *All's Well*: Judi buys champagne for the whole company, plus hangers-on like me.

There's a buzz in Stratford that I haven't known for years, an RSC buzz. This is partly because of Judi's return, and partly because Mike Boyd is working wonders. His first proper season starts in a few weeks, and it's exciting: the RSC will be an ensemble again, a proper ensemble, and there'll be a training course built into it, with John Barton and Peter Hall doing workshops, and, best news of all, there'll be a New Writing Festival, and this will be at the Other Place (the closing of which was the most painful of all Project Fleet's barmy schemes). It feels like we're back on our feet at last, and Judi's return is a fitting symbol.

Tonight she tells me she first came to Stratford in 1961 to play Anya in Michel Saint Denis' production of *The Cherry Orchard* with Gielgud, and the last time here was as Imogen in *Cymbeline* in 1979. I ask her what it's like to be back. 'Strange,' she says. 'Nice strange?' I ask. 'Everything,' she says simply. I don't need to ask more. This is where she and Michael Williams met, lived and worked together, and he's buried just a few miles away. The only time I've worked with Judi was on *Mrs Brown*, in which she played Queen Victoria during the prolonged period of her mourning after Albert's death; really a prolonged nervous breakdown. Judi played those moments with such truthfulness that I found them deeply upsetting to watch, but tonight her own, real mourning is strikingly different. Michael's presence is so powerful it's as though he's sitting next to her in the window table. It's not that she's solemn or sad – on the contrary, we never stop laughing – but you get the feeling that she's thinking of him constantly, always, without end. Greg says she brings this same sense of grief to the role of the Countess – as a permanent, almost peaceful thing – and that it's very fine.

Saturday 14th December 2003

Grayshott Hall Health Farm. The morning after *All's Well* pressed, Greg flew to Washington to open *Shrew* and John

Fletcher's 'sequel', *The Tamer Tamed*. So I've transferred my *Othello*-learning and *Primo*-writing here. I also have to lose some weight. It was a pleasure putting it on for Tsafendas, but it's a bugger shifting it for Iago.

I wrote *Primo* so long ago that I can't remember what's straight from *If This Is A Man*, and what's from elsewhere. Currently I'm inching through my text cross-checking it with Levi's. As I read the script I find myself holding my breath from time to time – *please God let this bit be from the book* – and nine out of ten times my prayers are answered. Where I've tinkered most is building up the characters of Alberto and Lorenzo. Levi writes them more fully in a later book, *Moments of Reprieve*, and I've used several sections from this. Discussing it with Jack Bradley, we've decided that I need to list every one of these insertions, and be completely open with the Estate about them. Now that we've won their trust, we must continue to earn it.

Inbetween today's sessions in the sauna and gym, I learned lines and wrote, and was completely exhausted when I went to bed. Was fast asleep when the fire bell went off and kept going. Dressed reluctantly, then stood in my room, not knowing what to do. (Why does one assume fire bells to be false alarms? Will one know the difference when the real thing occurs?) Wondering which of my possessions to take, I decided on just my briefcase, containing *Primo*, *If This Is A Man*, my diary, and the rave reviews for *All's Well*, which Greg hasn't seen yet. Needless to say, as soon as I got outside the ringing stopped.

Sunday 14th December 2003

Richard is here. Arrived late last night (after a speaking engagement at a London dinner) just at the time of the fire alarm, in fact. He couldn't hear it in the car park, so didn't know what was going on. As he headed towards the lobby with his luggage, a lot of guests in white gowns came running out. He wondered if Grayshott had instituted a new regime of midnight exercises.

More rave reviews for *All's Well* in the Sundays. I had the pleasure of waking Greg in Washington with the news.

During lunch, Richard and I became engrossed in a discussion about *Primo*. Richard was reading the Ian Thomson biography, and wanted to discuss Levi's death. There's something profoundly shocking and disappointing about the idea that he committed suicide. How could the great survivor kill himself? Imagine if Mandela did that. I told Richard about Carole Angier's theory in the other Levi biography. She thinks, yes it was suicide, but no it wasn't to do with Auschwitz. He was a depressive – before Auschwitz, after Auschwitz, but not *in* Auschwitz. At first this seems improbable, then it starts to make sense. Auschwitz lives up to his worst nightmares. The world really is as frightening and threatening as he'd pictured it in his dark moments. Everything is depressing, the place itself is like a giant manifestation of depression. So his energy switches into a fight for survival.

I said that I took comfort from this. I was still hoping to discover that Levi didn't commit suicide (why would a chemist, with access to numerous poisons, kill himself by jumping down a stairwell?), but if he did, I preferred the idea that it wasn't because of Auschwitz.

Richard and I were talking away, coming to the end of our second course, when he suddenly started jigging up and down in his seat. He'd phoned his sister Moira before lunch, and forgotten to tell me something: 'She thinks they've caught Saddam Hussein . . . !'

We dashed up to his room, put on Sky News, and to our astonishment there he was: dishevelled, bearded, dressed like an Iraqi villager, but unmistakably him – those eyes – him, not a double. An American army medic was examining his teeth with a torch, and then checking his hair for lice, handling him quite roughly. It was shocking and thrilling to see him like this. I suppose it touches a need in us all – to see the bad guy caught and shamed. And this was on a massive scale: an iconic Bad

Guy, a giant figure of evil power, the devil on earth. Yet here he was with a torch being shone in his mouth and his head shoved about. Whatever one's feelings about the war, this was good, this was justice. Imagine Hitler like this.

Tuesday 23rd December 2003

Greg is jet-lagged. He returned from Washington yesterday morning, and this evening we're flying to South Africa, where we'll spend Xmas and New Year with the family, before *Othello* starts in early January. I feel quite anxious about going home this time. I've been told to expect quite a change in Mom. But at least she seems to have a peaceful form of the illness – none of the aggression and violence you hear about, which must be unbearable. Mom just wants to stay in her bedroom all the time.

During this past week, I finished the new draft of *Primo*, and we've sent this to Roberto Gilodi in Turin, along with a letter from me detailing any additions from other sources. These are not many. The text is about 98% from *If This Is A Man*, 1% from *Moments of Reprieve*, and 1% from *The Truce*. But if the Estate won't allow the *Truce* material (the liberation of the camp; the section about shame), this will be a serious loss. As I worked on the draft, I still kept weeping all the time. I don't know how I'm going to perform it. But it's extraordinary material.

5th January–17th July 2004. These six-and-a-half months are the period of Othello, *and, as with* I.D., *it is too big a story to tell here. Once again, I'll represent it with just one key entry:*

Thursday 19th February 2004

It's the morning after press night of *Othello*. A sunny, icy Stratford day. The express train I've been on for the past seven weeks has come to a shuddering halt. Today is free. I've noth-

ing to do, and no-one to do it with. Greg had to dash back to
London first thing. Tonight he has another opening! The West
End transfer of *All's Well*. No work, no Greg. What else is there?

So how did last night go?

I'm afraid we didn't serve up the play as well as we can, and
have done in the rehearsal run-throughs and some of the previews. On those occasions, Sello and I achieved a chemistry
which felt tremendous: two men tumbling into hell, each dragging the other with him – Iago intoxicated by the joy-ride,
indifferent to his own fate, Othello bewildered, wild, dangerous – down they go, together they fall. Sello has achieved
heroic things with the role. He brings a natural African power
to it which you can feel onstage like a fire or hurricane. And
he's conquered the task of speaking the huge role not only in
English (which isn't his first language), but in Shakespearian
English . . . or almost conquered it. Last night he was a bit quiet
and tentative again. Elsewhere, the good performances remained
good – Lisa Dillon as Desdemona, Ken Bones as Brabantio,
Mark Lockyer as Roderigo, and especially Amanda Harris as
Emilia.

And me? I wasn't at all frightened beforehand, had a good
feeling, a sense I'd fly. Well, I didn't. Despite going through the
lines umpteen times yesterday, they began to slip and slide a
bit. Only tiny fluffs, but unsettling – the worst was on the line,
'Abuse him to the Moor in the rank garb', when 'Moor' came out
as 'Boor.' (Wait for the review that says, 'This South-African-
led production bizarrely substitutes "Boer" for "Moor".')
Basically I felt The Fear settle in – dry mouth, gabbling inner
voices – which was fucking unfortunate on this of all nights.
My performance became a question of survival rather than
achievement. In that sense, I succeeded – I got to the end in
one piece – but it's probably the lamest I've ever been in front
of the critics. Which is also fucking unfortunate, since I've felt
very proud of what Greg and I have done with Iago. We've said
bollocks to the 'motiveless malignity' theory (Coleridge was on

too much opium the day he coined that phrase), and we play the character clearly motivated by jealousy, a feverish sexual jealousy – based on the lines when he imagines that both Othello and Cassio are sleeping with his wife. The play is famously about one man possessed by jealousy; we're saying it's about two. Greg's special insight was to see Iago as the Great Improviser, always thinking on his feet, trying to keep one step ahead of the game, constantly risking exposure and punishment. My contribution was to play him as a die-hard RSM, right down to his square-bashing boots (based on those guys I knew and feared during my National Service in the South African army): rough, humorous, popular with the lads, happier at work than at home. On the outside he's totally trustworthy ('honest Iago'), on the inside (revealed in the soliloquies) he's severely disturbed.

Anyway, even during the previews, I wasn't sure the interpretation was quite coming across. Last night, even less so. Fuck it, fuck it, fuck it.

I don't look at reviews, but it's important to get a temperature reading, so both Greg and Paul Lyon-Maris mark them out of 10 for me.

Greg rings from London. Says there's a rave 10 in the Mail, rather disappointing 5's in the Guardian and Telegraph, something in the Standard that's so routinely rude it's not worth considering, and a very good 7 in the Independent, further boosted by a big article alongside, with the headline: 'Is Antony Sher the best interpreter of Shakespeare in the country?' Since I myself would answer, 'You've got to be joking', on this particular morning, it does nothing to lift my spirits. I can hear in Greg's voice that he's feeling bruised. He's had such a run of success in the classics over recent years – *Winter's Tale, Macbeth, the Jacobethans, Shrew, Tamer, All's Well* – he was bound to do one that isn't unanimously praised. Just a pity it's this one, which we've been planning for over a decade.

As the day progresses I get a series of aftershocks from last night – I can't believe I was so feeble, so nervous – and become increasingly anxious about doing the show again tonight. It really does seem that The Fear is settling in now, taking up residence. Tsafendas imagined he had a giant tapeworm living inside him, talking to him, driving him to murder. I picture my demon as a hyena, the ugliest animal in creation, with a snout that's permanently blackened with blood. This thing has its head in my guts now, and I don't know what to do.

The one thing I mustn't do is a solo show.

And yet a couple of nights ago, after the final preview, we got back to Avonside and heard an amazing message from Mic on the answerphone. Roberto Gilodi had just reported back that the Primo Levi Estate totally approved my script, including all the additions from *The Truce* and *Moments of Reprieve*. Primo's son Renzo, who's fluent in English, personally read the manuscript, and sent this message: 'My family give our blessing to this project.' After all we've been through with them, this touched me more than I can say. I saw it as a promising omen, the best good luck message anyone could give me before an important opening.

Yes well, today it feels like it didn't quite work out.

Thursday 22nd July 2004

Dear God, England in midsummer. We've just driven across London, and it could've been Delhi during a monsoon. Torrential rain, big drops clashing on the windscreen, sheets of white water leaping up from the road. And I'm ill. Ostensibly just a cold – a real stinker of a cold – but I know what this really is. PTSD. Post Traumatic Show Disorder.

Othello finally finished last Saturday night. Publicly it was a success. The reviews evened out strongly in our favour, and for five months we played to totally full houses, first in the Swan in Stratford, then on a tour round Japan, and then in London's new Trafalgar Studios (the old Whitehall Theatre), which we had the honour to open. But privately, as an actor, I've gone through a rough time. My battle with The Fear grew worse than I could've imagined. In an attempt to get me out of the situation, my body began to invent bizarre psychosomatic illnesses. During some performances in Stratford, I developed such bad stomach pains and nausea that I had to consult a gastro-enterologist and have a series of tests – nothing was found, of course. In Japan I experienced small but alarming losses of balance which threatened to tip me off the stage; the first time it happened I thought we were in an earthquake.

Again and again I came very, very close to doing what I called 'an Ian Holm' – walking offstage and huddling on the floor of my dressing room. (Holm did this during the final preview of the 1976 RSC *Iceman Cometh*.) But I somehow didn't. I knew that if I did, I'd never come back. (Which Holm has done, triumphantly.) So . . . for whatever reason . . . I got through it.

I was helped by my therapist, Marietta Young, whom I've continued to see weekly ever since I left the clinic for cocaine dependency in 1996. I do art therapy with her. Putting down images of things which trouble me helps to offload them. In this case, I drew an image of The Fear as a nightmarish hyena, and showed it slinking away. (In performance when The Fear visits, one of my inner voices shouts at it: Fuck off!) Marietta pointed out that I depicted it heading for the left of the page, and, since we write from left to right, this symbolised the past. So maybe I could put it behind me now. Although I've not managed that – not yet – I've certainly gained some strength from summoning up this image: the demonic animal getting the order to fuck off, and obeying it, hunched and cowed.

In the meantime, the start date of *Primo* draws closer: the workshop is just two weeks away. I find myself having discussions with Richard about the production (he's assembled a formidable team: Hildegard Bechtler designing, Paul Pyant lighting, Jonathan Goldstein composing), and I find myself learning the lines. But I never find myself seriously consider-ing scrapping this project. Why not? Greg put it like this today:

'*Primo* is too important for The Fear to get in the way.'

'What, more important than Shakespeare?' I asked defiantly, knowing I was talking to a Bard nut, an anorak.

'Yes,' he replied without hesitation; 'Yes!'

Anyway, who knows what's going to happen. For the moment I'm just ill, for real, with a bad cold – and PTSD. So for a day or two I'm going to collapse in bed and not think about anything at all . . .

Monday 26th July 2004

I gave my first performance as Primo Levi today.

It was at the funeral of Ethel de Keyser, who died last week. Ethel, who ran the Canon Collins Educational Trust for Southern Africa. Ethel dead? I can't absorb it. As several people said in the crowd outside Golder's Green crematorium, where the turn-out was immense: 'She's probably around here somewhere.' Since she was a rather short figure, this idea was feasible: she was just out of view, but buzzing round, introducing us all to one another, as she always did, sniffing the air for possible sponsors. In fact, as someone else said, she probably organised today's service herself; she would've never trusted anyone else to handle such an important event. What a lady. Ran the Anti-Apartheid Movement for ten years, then ran BDAF (British Defence and Aid Fund for Southern Africa), and then, after the fall of apartheid, transformed it into Canon Collins, which she ran till just ten days ago.

She came to see *Othello* earlier this month, and I gave her a lift home afterwards. As we parted, she presented me with a book by the Guyanese poet, Martin Carter, and implored me to look at page 14. The poem here carries the refrain, 'I do not sleep to dream, but dream to change the world.' This could be Ethel's motto – in terms of South Africa – or indeed her epitaph. At today's gathering, I learned that she gave copies of the same book to all her close friends in the weeks before her death, and each time it was with the urgent request: look at page 14. Did she have a sense of death? Did she want this to be her last message?

There were glowing tributes during the service: from the High Commissioner Lindiwe Mabuza, from Lillian Cingo (who'd flown over South Africa; she runs the Health Train there), and from many others. There was also much laughter: Ethel was a fearsome bully, though always and only in the cause of South Africa.

She was also an avid reader, and Primo Levi was one of her heroes. One of the last things she did was organise a Canon Collins fund-raising event for one of *Primo's* performances at the National. She won't be attending that now, so I read the section called 'A Good Day', in which the Primo and the other prisoners become aware of the arrival of spring, and by luck have enough to eat for once. It's about optimism in the face of adversity. Which is very Ethel de Keyser. As someone put it today, she's one of those people whose lives make a difference; she helped to build the New South Africa.

'I do not sleep to dream, but dream to change the world.'

Tuesday 27th July 2004

A long line-learning session on *Primo* this morning. They're going into my memory box with surprising ease. Why? Maybe because the original author's language is strong and strangely beautiful. (In that extract I read at Ethel's funeral yesterday, when they see the green meadows in sunshine, he writes: 'We look around like blind people who have recovered their sight, and we look at each other. We have never seen each other in sunlight.') And maybe because, although harrowing, the events grip you. You *have* to relate them accurately. He had to, and you have to.

Had a good long talk with Richard on the phone, about playing the actual role, which we haven't really discussed much.

I was struck by a different tone in his voice, something I've never heard before in all our years of friendship, something difficult to describe . . . a particular mixture of kindness and strength. He said he was going to help me reach so far inside the character that it won't be a question of acting, but *being*. I will absorb so much of the subject, he said, through the workshop, through the trips to Auschwitz and Turin which we're planning, that in the end it should feel more like my own experience than Primo's, and I should just *need* to tell people about it, barely aware of being in a theatre. He said, rightly, that an audience can smell authenticity when it comes to a subject like the Holocaust. It was really only this issue he was referring to, yet he seemed also to be addressing my stage fright, although I've never discussed it with him. It's as if he's somehow read my mind, or my diary, and is electing to cure me.

A fresh side of Richard is coming into focus. Him as a director. Although we've worked together in this relationship once before, on *Changing Step*, a BBC film that I wrote and he directed, I only gave myself a minor role in that, so I'm thinking of *Primo* as the first time. There's a different kind of warmth coming from Richard. As a friend, he's exceptionally generous, and very funny of course, but there's always something severe too, an austerity, a Calvinist streak – his Scottishness, I suppose. Added to that he lives alone and has no partner. Perhaps as a director he feels more complete: now he has a family, people who rely on him, and whom he leads. Today there was a new gentleness in him – that's the word, gentleness – which surprised and touched me.

Wednesday 28th July 2004

I've just had an extraordinary encounter in extraordinary circumstances.

To explain the circumstances first. Greg and I are among the guests at a three-day house party at Sandringham, hosted by Prince Charles and Camilla Parker-Bowles. Our friends were all very excited about us coming here, but we were just apprehensive. Turns out all the other guests felt the same. On the first evening – yesterday – I passed Jeremy Paxman in a corridor, and he said, 'I've just had a conversation with Prince Charles – about fishing – and everything I said seemed to echo in my head – I sounded like such an idiot.' Well, if Jeremy Paxman could sound like an idiot, I knew we were going to be OK. And of course our hosts are so accomplished at social skills that the atmosphere is totally relaxed and easy.

Nevertheless, it's a relief that the other guests include a couple of mates – the actress Miriam Margolyes, the playwright Peter Shaffer. Then there's one of my heroes, the artist David Hockney, also Lady Solti (widow of the conductor), Michael Morpurgo (the Children's Laureate), James Howard-Johnston and Angela Huth (the historian and the writer), Leo de Rothschild (of the banking family), Drue Heinz (of the beans empire), and the Earl and Countess of Gowrie. He was Arts Minister under Thatcher, then Head of the Arts Council, and it's she – Neiti – with whom I will have my extraordinary encounter.

This morning all of us accompanied Prince Charles and Camilla to the Sandringham Flower Show – all except Hockney, whom I watched crossing the great lawn at the back of the house with watercolour pad and paints. Then we travelled in a convoy of cars to an informal lunch at one of the log cabins dotted round the estate, used as rest places during the hunting and fishing seasons. The meal was described as a picnic, but was rather sumptuous, on a long table in the shade of a tree. Afterwards you could choose to either drive or walk back to the main house. We walked. It lasted about an hour and a half, through sunny fields and dappled woods, with Prince

Charles leading, carrying a tall walking staff – I suppose he knows his way round here better than anyone.

I fell in alongside Neiti Gowrie. She looks my age, but is maybe older; trim, with blonde hair, fine features, and a sense of grace. She asked me what I was doing, and I told her about *Primo:* the workshop starts next week, and on the first weekend Richard, Greg and I are flying to Poland to visit Auschwitz. As we talked I grew intrigued by her accent, and asked her about it.

'Well, I was born in Germany,' she replied.

'Oh,' I said; 'How long have you lived here?'

'Since just after the war.'

'Uh–huh.'

'I should also explain,' she said in a steady tone; 'That my father was in the SS.'

I went silent.

She continued, 'His name was Fritz–Dietlof von der Schulenburg. He was Prussian. And part of the group who tried to assassinate Hitler.'

I stopped walking. 'The group who planted the bomb?'

'Yes.'

'Under a table . . . in a briefing room . . . '

'At the *Wolfsschanze,* yes, the Wolf's Lair . . . well, I'm sure you know what happened.'

'I do.'

When the assassination attempt failed, Hitler had the conspirators executed – hanged with piano wire – and had this filmed, and watched it repeatedly. I glanced at Neiti. She looked composed, willing to talk on. I said: 'Your father did something very heroic, but I suppose not if you were in Germany. What was that like?'

'Well, I was only an infant, yet I do have some sense of the moment. And natually I've heard the family stories . . . my mother wrote these down actually . . . just for us . . . '

It was summertime, Neiti said, and they were staying in their lakeside home, Trebbelow, in Northern Germany. Neiti's father, Count von der Schulenburg, visited the family two days before the assassination attempt, which would fall on his wife's birthday. He told her what was going to happen, and they parted tenderly the following morning at the railway station. They would never see one another again. After the event, she was interrogated by the Gestapo. A gamekeeper had informed on the family, revealing that von Stauffenberg (the officer who actually took the bomb into the briefing room, concealed in his briefcase) was a guest at Trebbelow over Easter. Neiti's mother claimed complete ignorance of the plot. To try and save her husband's life, she travelled to Berlin to talk to Himmler (whom they knew), but he refused to meet her, and the execution went ahead. Neiti concluded:

'No, I don't think my mother had any sense of heroism. Not at the time. No – just of grief, and fear.'

'Yes of course,' I said.

'When we fled, we were picked up by the British, luckily, not the Russians.'

We walked on for a bit. Then I asked, 'What year was the assassination attempt?'

' '44.'

' '44? That's the year Levi is in Auschwitz.'

'Is it?'

'The book starts with that fact. An astonishing sentence – 'It was my good fortune to be deported to Auschwitz only in 1944.' There was a labour shortage in '44, so the Nazis were allowing the prisoners to live longer.'

'Ah yes.'

'It was summer, you say – the attempt?'

'It was July. The 20th of July. Just after 1pm.'

I nodded, lost in thought. Just after 1pm on the 20th of July 1944, when the bomb went off in the *Wolfsschanze*, von der Schulenburg was trying to kill Hitler, and would be executed for it, while at the same moment Primo Levi was probably on an afternoon work shift, trying to to survive Auschwitz, where conditions were relatively better because of the arrival of warmer weather (as he describes in 'A Good Day', which I read at Ethel's funeral on Monday).

I said to Neiti: 'I wonder if Levi and the others in Auschwitz heard what your father was part of, what he tried to do?'

'I wonder,' she said in a quiet voice, slightly tired. We passed on to other topics.

There have been many almost unreal moments during our visit, but none so more than this: during a sunny afternoon stroll somewhere on an estate owned by the British royal family, a momentary coming together of Primo Levi and an SS officer who plotted to kill Hitler.

This evening there's a formal and very romantic dinner in the garden of the house, under an avenue of lime trees, the long table lit by candles, with night-lights and lanterns in the branches and on the surrounding lawn. Afterwards, Miriam Margolyes volunteers to perform a short section of her one-woman show, *Dickens' Women*. Relieved that nobody is asking me to perform anything, and emboldened by a glass or two, I say to Prince Charles, 'Why don't you do the Spike Milligan poem you did at that RSC fund-raiser at Home House?' He looks at me with surprise. I think: *Ah yes, that's probably not the way you talk to royalty.* But then he pops into his study and returns saying: 'I haven't got that with me, but Barry Humphries gave me one of his monologues recently – I'll do that.' Barry Humphries? Are we going to see Prince Charles as Dame Edna? No. He does a Sandy Stone speech – in a very passable Australian accent, and with a sense of comedy that (almost) matches Miriam's turn as Mr and Mrs Bumble.

Afterwards, as Greg and I retire to our bedroom, I say:

'I can't really get my head round this – Sandringham one week, Auschwitz the next.'

Part Three

Preparing Primo

Monday 2nd August 2004

Today it begins. *Primo* begins today.

Although it's just a workshop for the next fortnight, we then segue straight into rehearsals – for another five weeks – so in effect a journey begins today which will end in two months' time with me standing on the stage of the Cottesloe and performing *Primo*.

Greg and I have a ritual when we start a new job, whether together or independently. While touring India in 1998 we bought a sizeable wooden Ganesh, and it now has pride of place on the mantelpiece in our dining room. Since this elephant-headed, multi-armed, dancing figure is known as the God of Good Beginnings, we mark each venture by taking out a little packet of vermillion powder (traditionally used for the bindi mark on the forehead), and throwing a pinch of it over him while making a silent wish. This morning, a fresh sprinkle of red – 'for *Primo*' – joined the aged colour that already adorns Ganesh, engrained into his folds and creases over the years . . . 'for *Winter's Tale* ' . . . 'for *Macbeth* ' . . . and so on.

At the National Theatre Studio in Waterloo, I'm intrigued to meet the rest of the cast – and there can't be many other one-man shows which allow you to say that. Richard has pursued his early idea of employing other actors for the workshop so we can do improvisations of some of Levi's ordeals in Auschwitz – only symbolically of course – and allow me to experience what Richard no longer calls 'humiliation' but 'punishment'. I'm extremely apprehensive about this. I've given up saying, 'But Richard why would I need punishment exercises when I've got *you* directing?' and I now say: 'I'm a gay Jewish white South African, what can you teach me about punishment?!' He never smiles. He's deadly serious about this.

There are four other actors. One other who's Jewish – Elliot Levey – and can therefore play another prisoner, and three who are fluent in German – Christoph Hülsen, Nick Fletcher, Rupert Wickham – and can play guards. In Auschwitz, one of the worst early experiences was trying to obey orders in a language you didn't understand.

Our workshop is in the Studio's main room, a vast indus-trial-like space which somehow feels conducive to the material we're investigating. We spend the morning with warm-up games and easy exercises: Richard wants to explore first-person narrative, so we tell some of our own life stories, and read pieces from the newspaper. Then in the afternoon we get our first heavyweight contribution. A visit from James Thompson, a clinical psychologist who specialises in trauma. He's worked on several of the British disasters of recent years, including the Bradford and King's Cross fires, and the sinking of the Marchioness. A quiet, humourous, delicately poweful man, he has fascinating tales and insights. I was very taken with this phrase: 'The risk of remembering.' Holocaust survivors seem to divide into two groups: those who won't say a word about what happened to them (often suffering nightmares and traumas in later life), and those who can't stop talking. Primo obviously falls into the second catergory. Both of his biographers (I'm currently reading the other one, by Ian Thomson) describe him as an exceptionally shy young man who hated public speaking, and yet after he got back from Auschwitz he turned into the Ancient Mariner, button-holing strangers in the street or on trains to tell them what happened to him. I'm taking comfort from this: he had his own version of The Fear, yet conquered it. Something more important was present.

When I pressed James Thompson on Levi's fatal fall down the stairwell of his home, and his condition as a manic depressive, he resisted this. He's a Levi fan, and didn't like the idea that the man should be remembered for his death. He spoke eloquently about this:

'What killed him? The stairwell killed him. Suicide can be a momentary choice. Let's not think of that. Let's think how well he survived, and what he achieved. Not just as a writer, but also as a chemist. He didn't commit suicide. He committed *life*.'

Our first day ended with us watching *I Remember*, a documentary by Spielberg and Wajda, in which survivors tell their stories, a mini *Shoah*. The first two men make strong impressions. Tragedy has filled them with a special stillness, a kind of grace. How *carefully* they remember, how rigorously they get their facts right. At certain painful moments, they suddenly stop, fight to control themselves, and always succeed. One man keeps having flash memories . . . you see him seeing them; they show in his eyes, as if flicked on by a switch . . . they silence him . . . he seems to weep without tears or noise, he weeps within . . . then he carries on.

Afterwards we went for a drink at the pub across from the Studio, The Windmill. I found myself sitting next to Christoph, who's the only genuine German among the German-speakers; he's in his mid-twenties, tall, gentle. I said, 'Is this difficult for you? In just one day, we've already heard so many anti-German remarks, either directly or by allusion.'

He replied, 'It's not anti-German. It's anti-Nazi.'

'Yes of course – I'm sorry – I'm just showing my own prejudice.'

By the time I got home, I was absolutely whacked. In bed by ten.

Tuesday 3rd August 2004

Everyone's reading Holocaust books, and at a certain point each day Richard invites us to share relevant pieces with the group. The session is called Nuggets. This morning, Rupert reads a particularly shocking account of torture and its sexual side. I wonder where on earth he'd found it. Is this someone's confession at the Nuremberg trials? Turns out it's from Ariel Dorfman's play *Death and the Maiden*, which Rupert is currently performing at the King's Head.

Then we work on an exercise which Richard's calling Testimonies. He hands out short extracts from real survivors. We each practise our piece, first on our own, then to someone else, then to the group. It's good to be sharing my basic problem – how to deliver this kind of material – with other actors. I learn from watching them, from their mistakes (over-demonstrative, over-emotive) and their successes (stillness, conviction). The National's renowned voice coach, Patsy Rodenburg, is present, and as always she has words of wisdom: 'You have to know these things so deeply you don't embellish them. They're just in every atom of you.'

Because so much of our work is focused on dark and ugly things, Richard has also instituted a daily game. Called Fourball, it's played round a gaffer-taped square on the floor, divided into four sections. There's a king on one corner, three other players, and a referee (ie. whoever's currently knocked out of the action). Using a beach-ball, the king serves and then he and the others try to keep it bouncing from square to square with deft nudges of the hand. It's so simple that even I, who grew up hating games in sports-mad South Africa, can keep up. Much laughter, much release of tension.

Talking of South Africa, our producer Pádraig Cusack popped down from the National today with good news. We can do *Primo* in Cape Town. From the start of this project, I've dreamed of performing it there – I've never played my home-town, and *Primo* is an ideal debut – but there's been difficulty raising the money. Anyway, the Baxter Theatre is definitely proceeding now, and they've scheduled the run for January next year. I'm going to be taking *Primo* home.

Wednesday 4th August 2004

Wake very uneasy.

Today we're doing the first punishment exercise – 'The Transport' – a version of the train journey to Auschwitz. Apparently, the Studio tried to find a cattle truck (!), but failed, and so we're using some NT vehicle. Elliot and I will be locked inside and driven around. I keep trying to have a dicussion about ground rules, but Richard keeps resisting. Insists he's got to be able to surprise me. (Much of the terror which Primo and the others experienced was not knowing what would happen next.) I, in turn, insist there have to be boundaries. As recent events in Iraq's Abu Ghraib jail showed, the quickest and most effective way of humiliating prisoners is through nudity and sex. I'm making both of these out of bounds. Along with physical violence. And prolonged hunger and thirst.

So what's left?

At the Studio, we begin by looking at Ian Thomson's account of Primo's train journey, taking turns to read page by page. I find it very upsetting. People trying to slake their thirst by licking the condensation on the pipes, only to have their tongues stick fast to the freezing metal. The lack of even a bucket as a toilet . . . what Levi calls the humiliation of violated modesty.

I've barely caught my breath from this shocking material when we're into our own symbolic version.

Richard briefs the two groups separately: the prisoners and the guards. With us – Elliot and me – he gives a vague indication of the sequence of events without any details. Says we can say 'Stop' at any point, and while in the back of the truck we can bang on the partition to the driver and he'll immediately pull over. But Richard asks us to stay in character as far as possible.

Obviously if this exercise is to serve any purpose I have to enter into it fully. I once did a Mike Leigh play, so I've learned how to press the button, and commit to this kind of improvisation – it's like a form of self-hypnosis. There's a public perception that actors bring their characters home with them, which I've never believed is true, but the work we're about to do is the closest coming together of acting and reality that I know. I feel an acute sense of anxiety.

Elliot and I now wait at the far end of the big room, in separate corners, facing the wall, our luggage at our side. Nazi military music is put on. We hear the guards enter, chatting in German. Then it starts. They chase us into the centre, get us to form up, about-turn and march off . . . none of this clear because of the language barrier . . . them swearing at us all the time, variations of 'Juden, Juden'. The convoy walks from the Studio to the NT, discreetly maintaining its shape in public. (But in fact, I already feel hypnotised: Waterloo looks unfamiliar, the passers-by look hostile.) At the NT, we're made to stand facing a wall again, while they fetch the truck: one that's normally used for transporting costumes. We're chased into it, and the closing mechanism whirrs and buzzes until it's sealed. I can't see the air vent, and start to panic – 'How do we breathe in here?' 'It's OK', Elliot says, pointing to the vent. I notice he's pale, and not smiling. (Elliot always smiles.) The experience has already been alarming . . . our total loss of power and comprehension . . . and the 'Juden' insults . . . these really get to me . . .

We're driven around for about three quarters of an hour, rattled about in the closed, stuffy space which is not meant for passengers; you have to clutch onto the ribbing of the walls. There's an opaque roof which occasionally shows the shadows of trees, or goes dark as we travel through underpasses. Although it's uncomfortable, I don't want the journey to finish – I get nervous when we pause at traffic lights – I don't know what's in store at the other end. (Describing the arrival at Auschwitz, Primo records: 'We wait for something which will certainly be terrible.') Finally the truck stops – we're chased out – it's the Studio's car park – we stand facing a wall for twenty minutes or so, while the guards drink water (it's a hot day) and mock us. Then we're chased back onto the truck, sealed in again, and rattled around for another half hour. When we stop next, and are chased off, we find ourselves back in the big room at the Studio. We're pushed into a corner, we stand there, a bell rings, and then Richard says, 'That's it, thank you.'

By now I've had, in every sense, a bad trip – I'm aware that no serious abuse occurred, yet I've gone to some bad places in my head. The exercise may have barely scratched the surface of any Auschwitz experience, but unfortunately it took me back to some troubled times in my own life: times when I was bullied at school and in the army (the Afrikaans word 'Jood' is uncomfortably close to the German), and times in the cocaine clinic too; times when I've felt genuinely vulnerable, powerless, frightened.

Today the overwhelming sensation was of shame – a very Primo Levi word – the shame of being a prisoner, a slave, a piece of shit, a Jew. Elliot and I could barely meet one another's eye, even when alone in the back of the truck, and we hardly ever spoke – just 'Are you alright?' when we both began pouring with sweat in that sweltering space. I'm beginning to understand why Levi says that in Auschwitz everyone was 'ferociously alone'. When you're scared and threatened, you close up rather than reach out. It's horrible to see a reflection of your own terror in someone else's cowed face, so you try not to look at them. You retreat far into yourself, and for me this took me into a dark corner where I'm just a small, useless creature.

After shame, the main feeling was of anger – I hated people treating me like that.

I suppose my anger is also half-aimed at Richard for cooking up the whole bloody idea. At the debriefing, he asks if we managed to stay in character throughout. I snap back: 'Of course not. If we're to use this exercise properly we have to go back into our own memories and feelings. I can't go via Primo's. I have to access my own experiences of humiliation and fear, and unfortunately I can do that rather easily.'

But as we talk on, I calm down – realising that the rest of the group have their own important contributions to make – and things become normal again.

So was it valuable?

Probably.

But I dread the thought of the next one . . .

Thursday 5th August 2004

This morning, two more punishment exercises:

First is 'The March to Work'. Elliot and I circle the big room again and again in time to march music, wearing shoes that approximate to the real thing – with wooden soles – which weigh down your feet, and make an odd clippity-cloppity noise. Your gait is dragging, your arms are held rigidly at your sides, your head is bowed, humbly, eyes fixed on the ground. (Levi talks of the prisoners marching 'with an odd, embarrassed step'.) The guards stand in the middle chatting to one another in German, and don't harass us, thankfully. Richard keeps this going for about twenty minutes, and by the end I'm wet with sweat again.

In the second, 'Work', Elliot and I are each given a task of manual labour: he moves ammunition cartridges from one end of the room to the other, and I move bricks. At one point, Elliot angers the German sergeant (Nick) and is made to do the

Lager squat: you hunker, you hold your arms out in front of you, and then stay like that. At another point I'm hauled over to a visiting SS officer (Christoph) and have my teeth and fingers examined, them handling me like an animal and saying something about Jewish teeth, Jewish fingers. Like yesterday, I find that I enter into the situation completely: the room ceases to be the Studio, the others cease to be fellow actors, Richard ceases to be Richard. I'm just in some terrible place where I've lost everything, and am worthless, and feel overwhelming shame. Afterwards, I urgently write down these notes:

– I hate my fear. It's not like The Fear. It's worse.

– I hate the sound of my voice muttering, 'Jawohl, jawohl', to every incomprehensible order (as they had to do in Auschwitz) – it's quiet and thin, not like my voice at all, or anyone's voice; it's the voice of a slave, a non-person.

– When the Germans pick on Elliot, I feel two things: relief that's it's not me, and concern for his safety. But relief most of all – thank God it's him, not me.

– Like yesterday, I'm caught in a circle. These exercises are meant to give me some feel of Auschwitz. But that's impossible, even symbolically. All they do is awake emotional recall and crash into my own bad memories. Yet that's good. Good for playing Primo.

This afternoon began with a game of Four-ball. I don't know if it's because of the punishment exercises, but I was suddenly playing with new aggression and competitiveness – me, the all-time non-sporty wuss – and thoroughly enjoying it.

Then a survivor came to speak to us. Josef Perl, aged 74, born in Czechoslovakia, arrested in 1940 aged 10, spent the rest of the war in various camps, including Auschwitz. He has a thick-set build, with big eyes behind spectacles, and one leg that he can't bend (because of a bullet wound during his

incarceration) propped on a case. He launched into his story –
one that he'd clearly told many times – speaking in a loud
insistent tone, a kind of wail, and maintaining this for over an
hour: a raging monologue. Yet its tone was in notable contrast
to the experiences he was relating, which sometimes sounded
quite fantastical.

He was, and is, deeply religious. During question time I
asked him to comment on Primo Levi's famous statement:
'There was Auschwitz, therefore God cannot exist.'

He replied angrily: 'Don't blame God! Where were the
human beings in those terrible places? God gave human beings
ten commandments. If human beings just kept half of them,
we'd be OK!'

Someone else asked if he'd ever returned to Auschwitz:

'I couldn't – I'd go mad, there's no inch of ground that isn't
soaked with Jewish blood. I couldn't step on that ground – I
would go mad!'

His rage is what I'll remember most.

Friday 6th August 2004

We began with a group discussion about Josef Perl's visit. I
confessed that I felt bad about saying this, but some of his
accounts sounded exaggerated to me. Others agreed. Nick got
angry: 'Who on earth are *we* to sit in judgement of *him*?!' Patsy
Rodenburg offered a possible explanation: Josef Perl had en-
dured terrible things at a very young age, so maybe his story
sometimes represents a child's-eye view of events, with strange
coincidences and feats of heroism. In itself it's evidence of a
badly maimed adolescence, and all the more moving for it. We
ended up having a very good talk, with everyone joining in
passionately. (I'm touched by the input from the other actors,
given that they're not working towards an end result as I am.)
Richard concluded by observing that Josef Perl was the complete opposite of Primo Levi. Levi is cool, almost detached,

while Perl is still white-hot with anger. When we asked Perl if he could forgive the Germans, he exploded, 'Who am I to forgive? If they want forgiveness, let them go ask God!' Levi on the other hand – with no God to turn to – does forgive.

This was a fitting moment to do our first reading of *Primo*. I just listened with Richard and Patsy, while the other four actors shared the text between them. They were excellent and so was the piece: powerful, fascinating, moving. I take no credit for this. It's pure Primo Levi.

(The other day his Estate contacted the National, to ask that his name be bigger than mine in the programme. I said fine, I'm not going to argue about billing with Primo Levi.)

After the reading, Patsy was very encouraging about the script, and I value her opinion. I said to Richard, 'The only major problem I can detect at this point is that there's only one laugh.' (Templer, the prisoner who can empty his bowels at will.) He replied, 'We'll see about that,' and a twinkle returned to his eye – it's been absent during some of the grimmer sessions over the last few days.

But all in all, a terrific first week. Even though the punishment exercises are disturbing, to put it mildly, they are indisputably valuable. The mere fact that I hate going where they take me – those bad inner places – means that I might have avoided them. And I can't. This is going to have to dig deeper than anything else I've done.

We retired across the road to the pub. The group have got three days off now while Richard and I fly to Poland.

'We're going to Auschwitz for the weekend . . . ' I said, then hesitated; 'Why does that sound wrong?'

'I've noticed the same thing all week,' said Nick; 'You can't put the word Auschwitz into any sentence without it sounding wrong.'

'Except this one,' said Elliot: 'Auschwitz was a tragedy.'

Saturday 7th August 2004

Kraków, Poland. During our visit to Auschwitz we're staying at the Holiday Inn – *this sentence definitely sounds wrong* – and by chance it's the same hotel where Previ Levi stayed on the second of his return visits. On his first visit in 1965 he only went to Auschwitz I, the main camp, and was dismayed and angered by the cleanliness of it, the trees and grass; it bore no resemblence to what he'd known. But when he came back in 1981 he went to Auschwitz II, Birkenau, and this shook him terribly: this was very similar to the camp where he was incarcerated, Auschwitz III, Monowitz, which no longer exists.

Tomorrow's tour will be my second visit too and I'm not looking forward to it. Last time it upset me badly. Thank God Greg has come along on this one. You need someone to hold.

Sunday 8th August 2004

A beautiful day. During the hour's drive from Kraków, the Polish countryside is sunny and green and heavy with summer. The world could not look safer. Yet I have a terrible feeling of dread. Like in that first improvisation last week, 'The Transport', I don't want us to reach our destination.

And this is in a comfortable car with a driver (the National and Holocaust Educational Trust have made the arrangements between them); imagine if you'd just spent several days crammed in a railway wagon, in freezing cold, with no water to drink, and everyone's shit heaped in the corners.

We arrive at the small Polish town of Oświęcim (Auschwitz in German) just after 10am, and make our way to the site, officially called the State Museum of Auschwitz-Birkenau. As you drive in, all you see at first is the brick building of the museum. To my surprise the car park is already almost full with tourist coaches and other vehicles. When I visted before it was in the winter months, and much quieter. At first I feel resentful about the presence of so many people – I want us to be here on our own – but then I have second thoughts. Primo devoted his life to making sure that no-one forgot Auschwitz. It's good that people come here, flock here in large numbers. The museum/camp is not easy to reach, so you have to make a determined effort. There's a lot of controversy about this place, the fact that it sells food and drink, and films for your camera, and everyone's snapping and videoing away. Well I'm sorry, but isn't that good too? Wouldn't Primo approve? Wouldn't he have said: yes go there, see it, photograph it, *remember it.*

When Greg and I were in Japan the first time, in 2000 with *Macbeth*, we visited Hiroshima: their museum, and peace park, and the one building which survived the blast. I think if everyone in the world visited Hiroshima and Auschwitz, we might make it a safer place.

On the other hand, does everyone come to these places for the right reason? Today, as we go into the entrance hall of the museum, Greg notices a piece of graffiti on the wall. Someone has drawn a swastika. Someone else has scored it out with violent strokes, gouging into the brick.

At the information desk, our contact is waiting: Krzysztof Antończyk, one of the top historians here – Head of Digital Archives – a quiet, neat figure in a light beige suit, fluent in English. He's going to be our guide for the day. He wants to explain the lay-out of the original camp, so we jostle through the crowds back to the car park, where the big aerial maps are located. As we go, I ask:

'How long have you worked here?'

'Ten years.'

'Ten. Forgive me, but isn't it depressing?'

'It was at first. After the first three months, I didn't think I could take any more. But you get through that. It was important, you see. I lost three of my family here.'

'So . . . you're Jewish?'

'No, they were partisans.'

'Ah. Like Primo Levi.'

'Exactly.'

I feel we're in safe hands. He knows that Levi felt he came here as a political prisoner first, a Jew second. As a non-believer, Levi had not chosen to be Jewish, but he had chosen to fight the fascists.

The aerial maps reveal something I hadn't appreciated before. What's known as Auschwitz was in fact a vast network of separate camps. The town, Oświęcim, is slapbang in the middle, so those citizens would have been hard-pressed to trot out the old excuse: 'We didn't know what was happening.' What was happening invaded their space every day: it was, in every sense, under their noses. Levi's camp Monowitz is to the south of the town, and some distance away from the *Judenramp* (Jewish platform), which is to the north, and where his transport arrived. After surviving the first selection alongside the train, he describes being driven in a lorry to Monowitz. Krzysztof says we'll do that journey later. Although Monowitz has reverted to being a village, there are still fragments of the camp, and he wants us to see them.

Now we struggle through the crowds again, heading for the main camp, Auschwitz I. I know what's coming, and brace myself, taking hold of Greg's arm. You leave the museum building, turn a corner, and suddenly it's there. The gate. The *Arbeit Macht Frei* gate. Like when I was here last, something seems to come up through the ground and shake me. I start crying, I feel scared, lost, defenceless. The most unsettling thing is how small and ordinary the gate is. Because of its reputation you expect something on a monstrous scale, towering upwards, throwing a giant, sinister shadow. In reality it's a gate, just a gate – talk about the banality of evil – just high and wide enough for a military truck. Yet, as Krzysztof mentions, 'There was a saying in the Lager: "You come in through a gate, you go out through a chimney".'

When I calm down, we take some photographs. This is precisely the kind of thing that horrifies some people: *Visitors pose
under the Arbeit Macht Frei sign . . . !* Yes well sorry, but we're
here to work, and we might need these shots for reference.

Once we're through the gate, I don't really know how to
record the rest. So I'm just going to reproduce the notes I made
as Krzysztof took us round Auschwitz I:

Just inside the gate, the site where the little band played
as the prisoners marched to and from work; against a big
wooden hut.

All other buildings are brick, but when originally built –
as Polish military barracks, pre-war – they were covered
with plaster. The SS made the first prisoners strip off this
plaster, but gave out no tools. They had to do it with
spoons and fingernails.

A tree where recaptured escapees would be exhibited
with a sign round their necks: 'Hooray we're here again.'
Then they were hanged.

Krzysztof: 'You can't use logic here . . . it's a unique
place . . . an island far away from the world.'

There was a swimming pool (really just a small reser-
voir, but with steps down into the water) where the SS
made prisoners hold swimming races. There were also
boxing and football matches. SS boredom was a factor
here.

Winters very cold, summers very hot, the winds very
strong – Auschwitz is on a flat plain.

Paperwork bizarre. Constant cover-up. Why? If you
believe that Jews, gays, Communists, gypsies, etc. are low-
life worthy of extermination, why all the code? (Young
deaths are recorded as 'heart attacks'. Victims of the selections require 'special treatment'.) Why bother? Aren't the
SS expecting to win the war?

Krzysztof: 'Everything is upside-down here . . . in the hospitals, the doctors are killing the patients . . . '

While the selection is happening on the train platform, veteran prisoners whisper to young mothers: 'Give baby to grandparents, don't ask why.' Babies & grandparents are automatically heading for the gas chambers, but a young woman on her own could survive (maybe assigned to the Auschwitz brothel).

A large white plaster model of the lay-out of the gas chamber & ovens. Krzysztof: 'In the changing rooms, the clothes hooks had numbers. You'd be told to remember yours, so there wouldn't be a mix-up after the showers.'

A cabinet of Zyklon B canisters and the pebble-like crystals – originally just a disinfectant. It took many tests to get the lethal dosage right – during these tests people took days to die.

Ovens – healthy bodies burn faster – all the fat – just 15 mins. – thin skeletal bodies can take up to an hour.

A colossal glass cabinet of human hair – it stretches across the whole room. Krzysztof: 'The museum used the wrong preservative originally – that's why all the hair is the same grey colour now – originally it would've been black, brown, red.' All grey now – as though the hair has aged after its owners died. Greg & I are crying again here.

Hair is used in products. Shoulder padding in jackets. A roll of canvas-like material; on the edge, little strands of someone's hair.

We go outside – the museum displays are in different barracks – the fresh air and sunshine comes as a shock. You reel about. You can't absorb the good world.

Giant cases of combs, toothbrushes, clothes. The one of artificial limbs – legs and hands – stops me in my tracks. Half-human shapes.

An entire hill of dusty suitcases. Foul beauty. Can't help thinking of this as a set for *Godot* or some modern art installation, a Turner Prize winner. One case has 'Levi' (a common name) daubed on it in white paint – to prevent a mix-up after the showers.

A case of children's shoes – melted with age – and their small clothes. Greg is crying again.

Krzysztof: 'Corpses were carried to roll-call parade. The SS were very fussy about numbers. If someone died in your hut at night it didn't matter – the number of occupants had to be the same this morning as it was last night.'

The milling crowds of visitors in these rooms are peculiar & add to the oppressive, suffocating feel, but it's good, good they're all here. The people are hushed, shocked, pale. It's not like they're at the Acropolis or Big Ben.

On the other hand . . . someone's mobile rings . . . and the cunt takes the call.

The case of badges: yellow (Jewish), red (Communist), green (common criminal), pink (gay), and many, many others. My kind had their own special one. A pink triangle inverted over a yellow triangle – a gay Star of David. I'd've been here accused on 2 counts.

Walls and walls of identity pictures. Prisoners were photographed 3 times – profile, full face, three-quarters. Some try to smile politely. Some defiant. Most just dazed.

A big blow-up photo: a child – a girl – a Mengele experiment. It gets me, it winds me. Her huge black eyes are filled with an incredible amount of experience and grief. The expression isn't just adult, it's ancient. She's 2 years old and she's seen everything, knows everything. I photo it (how tasteless) to sketch later.

Krzystof: 'The reason Dr Mengele was so interested in twins is that he thought if he could just unlock the secret of how to make them, he could double the population of Germany overnight.'

This is a visit to hell.

Suffocation cells, standing-only cells, starvation cells.

Outside again, at the Wall of Death, where prisoners were shot. Piles of flowers and tributes here, including chains of coloured paper birds – cranes – from Japan. Created in memory of one of the victims of Hiroshima – a girl called Saduko – I remember her story – she made paper chains like these in hospital while she was dying.

Here's also the torture post. Your hands are tied behind you, a fastening attached, you're hoisted just off the ground, shoulders twisted backwards, aching, burning, fucked.

We pass the main gallows – which could take 12 at a time – and then see a single one. Here we get the first good news. This is where the Commandant of Auschwitz, Hoess, was brought back after the Nuremberg Trials & hanged. Just yards from his villa. This whole place makes any discussion about the death penalty completely redundant.

The last, worst thing. The gas chamber. Converted into an SS air-raid shelter towards the end, so it still stands. (They blew up the one at Birkenau.) Krzysztof: 'The chamber could take 700 people at a time.' I feel seriously alarmed going inside with today's crowds. A sign outside the door – 'Silence Please, Out Of Respect' – but we're too many to notice – most people don't even see it. The guides are the most disrespectful, shouting to their groups. But then for a moment it clears and our little party are here alone. It's the ugliest place on earth. The black stains on the thick, thick walls – are they of soot, damp, death? Next door, the room with the ovens is even worse. Outside I gasp at the air like I've just surfaced from drowning.

After this tour of Auschwitz I, it's a comfort to return to the museum building with its everyday features, its reception desk, its bookshop and canteen. We're all very silent. Krzysztof leads us to his car and invites us to climb in. We're going to trace the journey Primo made on arrival, from the location of the

Judenramp to Monowitz. It's a 15 minutes drive, and takes us through the centre of Oświęcim. The normality here looks as strange as the insanity we've just been studying.

Monowitz supplied slave labour to the neighbouring IG Farben rubber factory, and I'm surprised to see there's still an industrial complex here (I don't know what it produces now), and is still surrounded by its WWII perimeter: heavy grey concrete walls with those sinister hunched lamps. The camp itself has all but vanished. There's just one barracks remaining, and someone's converted it into their farm storehose. The whole place is just a rural village again, with single-storied houses and smallholdings. Goats and ducks shelter in the shade of trees, standing very still, watching us pass. We don't see a single person. A curious atmosphere. Maybe just because it's a hot Sunday afternoon. But Krzysztof says the locals aren't overjoyed about their history, and don't welcome visitors. At the far end we discover a small, odd monument: a Christian cross and a slab 'in memory of people murdered here 1941-1945.' Krzysztof points out that from here you can see a tall narrow building inside the factory compound; the 'Tower of Babel' which Primo refers to, a place he helped to build.

On the drive back, I notice two other views that Primo mentions on the daily march to work: to one side the Carpathian Mountains, to the other the town of Auschwitz (Oświęcim) with its steeple. In typical Primo style, he writes, 'A steeple here?' I ask Krzysztof about Oświęcim's Jewish population. He says it was considerable before the war; during it, some ended up in the camps next door; and afterwards – 'Yes, there was one Jew living here, but he died four years ago.'

We visit Birkenau next. Here the gate *is* big: built for a train to come through. Above it, there's a commanding view from the guard tower. It's very bleak. A flat expanse with the railway line down the centre, rows of brick huts to the left, wooden ones to the right, and in the far distance the ruins of the cremato-rium. As we make our way down the narrow stairwell, a group of young Israeli guys wearing yamulkas push their way up. Their silence is particular.

Krzysztof takes us into one of the wooden barracks (originally built as stables) which still contain the tiers of shelf-like bunks which prisoners shared, two-apiece, sleeping head to foot. Krzysztof: 'The diet of soup made them urinate again and again through the night. So they were climbing over one another all the time. There was no toilet in here, just a bucket, which quickly filled. There was no floor either – just mud, water and human waste.'

We can't take much more. It's a relief when Krzysztof says he's run out of time. (We've been here six hours.) As we walk back to the car, I ask him a last question, one that's been haunting me:

'Right at the end, when the Germans flee the camp, and Primo Levi can't join the Evacuation March . . . '

'He was ill, I think.'

'He had scarlet fever, that's right – he was in the infirmary, Ka-Be. Now the Germans know the Russians are about to arrive. And you've shown us today how paranoid they are about covering up all evidence. I mean, before fleeing, they blow up the crematorium over there. And then they take all the prisoners who can walk along with them – twenty thousand people – and even though they're going to murder most of them along the way it's still a massive operation. So why leave a few alive in the infirmary? Why not kill them too? In the book, Primo records that the patients think they're going to be killed. Why didn't the SS do it? It would've been so easy – bang, bang, bang. I can't understand it.'

'Oh well it's very simple,' says Krzysztof in his light precise and sober tone, 'and very banal, I'm afraid. Of course the SS were planning to kill them. They just ran out of time.'

This stuns me almost more than anything else we've learned today. If the Germans had just five minutes to spare before they left, we would have nothing of Primo Levi now, none of his Holocaust testimony, none of his other writings, not a word. He would be as silent and anonymous as all the other dead people surrounding us.

We thank Krzysztof – he's been a fine guide – and say goodbye. We're all subdued during the drive back to Kraków. Ordinary life looks surreal after Auschwitz. Someone mentions we forgot lunch, and we've had nothing to eat since this morning. A small, unintentional, apt gesture.

Back at the Holiday Inn, it's alcohol that's most urgently required. Richard has a beer, while Greg and I throw back large Polish vodkas. We try to debrief in the bar, but it's difficult. The day has been overwhelming. Richard's face carries an expression of profound tiredness. Greg can't stop crying. He says: 'I felt so angry in that place. I hate what we did to ourselves there.'

I say, 'Who's "we"?'

He and Richard answer in unison: 'We – us – human beings.'

Monday 9th August 2004

Our flight isn't till later, so we have the morning in Kraków. Its main square is spectacular: the biggest medieval square in Europe, dominated by the long Cloth Market building down the centre. When we came here after yesterday's visit, it was full of milling crowds; obviously a gentle perambulation is popular here on sunny Sunday evenings. In one area an impromptu audience were gathered round a group of young male buskers who had set up a ghetto-blaster and were doing solo turns: handstands, cartwheels, break-dancing. Stripped to the waist, they were very sexy, very fit, and so full of joy and energy it was hard to believe they were the same species of life as the figures we'd seen earlier in the archive photographs.

This morning it's a pleasure to forget about our project altogether, and to sit in cafés, to stroll and shop. All the stalls sell amber, carved into every possible object – necklaces,

cufflinks, crucifixes, figurines – or just sold as little glowing
stones. The more expensive ones hold tiny prehistoric insects
within. I'm reminded of my last visit to this part of the world,
in 1992, to Lithuania – where my family originally came from
– and of wandering along the Baltic one morning, picking up
raw amber from the shore . . .

Tuesday 10th August 2004

Back in London, back at the NT Studio.

We start with a meeting about the actual production: Richard,
me, Hildegard Bechtler (Designer), Jason Barnes (Cottesloe
Production Manager). Hildegard is short, attractive, warm.
She's also German, and it's one of the reasons Richard chose
her – which intrigues me. She shows a model of the set. A
brutal concrete chamber with a lead floor. Nothing in it except
one wooden chair. It's very simple and very powerful: a combination which maybe defines her as a designer. At the initial
design meeting, Richard said the set needed to have 'a cruel
beauty', and this is exactly what she's produced. At the
moment there are two doorways. Even though these just lead
to other chambers and the whole atmosphere is very claustro-
phobic, we decide that I need to be even more trapped. Hildegard suggests sealing up the smaller door. Perfect. Another
designer might've just removed it – she leaves it there, but seals
it, which is immediately more disturbing. The place is unspecific (it's perhaps 'the big empty room' into which Levi's
transport is herded on arrival), but its thick, ugly, stained walls
remind me of the gas chamber we saw on Sunday. I show
Hildegard our photographs. She's astonished by the resemblance. I'm about to say, 'Racial memory?' – but stop myself,
thank God. This project is unleashing some very sick humour.

It's laugh or cry, I suppose. I'm surprised by the shots of me
in our Auschwitz photos: I look older, thinner, ill. When the

other actors arrive, we show them the photos, the maps and books that we bought there, and try to describe the whole experience. It's difficult. I feel quite low throughout the day's work: doing more Testimonies, each of us taking turns to perform them.

One of the perks of this workshop for the other actors is that they're getting a Richard Wilson masterclass in acting. As a director he's much loved by actors, even though he's tough and rigorous – merciless, you could say. He watches you like a hawk, pouncing on any stray gesture or inflection. His favourite word is 'open' – as in 'Could you be more open in that section' – which basically means doing nothing, or rather doing everything but not letting it show. As in real life, when we constantly conceal more than reveal. Actors like to show, to do, to demonstrate, and my critics would certainly say I'm inclined this way. I've said to Richard that I want him to push me hard when we get into rehearsals, I want him to take my acting to places other directors cannot reach.

The day ended, as usual, with watching videos. First there's another documentary on Auschwitz (I felt like shouting, 'I don't want to go there again!'), and then *The Truce*, that film of Levi's book which Francesco Rosi managed to make with the blessing of the Estate. It opens where *Primo* ends, with the four Russian soldiers on horseback slowly appearing 'between the grey of the snow and the grey of the sky', and the liberation of the camp. In Levi's account, the atmosphere was flat and numb, with both sides – the liberators and liberated – overwhelmed by shame. But this version, being a *movie*, shows the prisoners dancing out of the camp, hugging one another, squealing, 'We're free, we're free!' And they're all rather clean and robust, and their striped uniforms have come straight off hangers in the Costume truck. I wanted to throw up.

Wednesday 11th August 2004

We had most of today off in preparation for an improvisation at the Studio this evening, when we'd work into the early hours, simulating nightime conditions in the camp. Richard suggested I might like to eat very little during today, or even fast completely. I thought this was going too far, particularly since I'm already dreading tonight, so I had a big lunch, and a long siesta afterwards. I still feel in shock from the visit to Auschwitz. It's a pity that there's been no real recovery time, and a pity that we go straight into rehearsals next week. I feel a repeat of the *I.D.* experience starting up, where the workload threatened to overwhelm me.

We assembled at the Studio at seven, and while waiting for darkness to fall, did readings, watched videos, and played Four-ball.

The 'Night' impro lasted about three hours, and went like this: Elliot and I were made to stand on the roll-call square for a long time in the dark (the guards had torches), then we were put in our hut, given a meagre soup and bread ration, allowed to sleep – on the floor, with a hard bundle of belongings as pillows – and then there was a rough wake-up call, and a long stand on the roll-call square again.

It wasn't as bad as the previous exercises, because of a new crucial factor. Companionship. I know I said before that fear and danger makes you withdraw from others, and develop the 'ferocious' aloneness which Primo describes in the Lager, but tonight Elliot and I were left on our own for long stretches of time, and drew comfort from talking. Primo and Alberto did the same thing – in fact, they teamed up so strongly, they defied the system. Elliot and I didn't attempt to be Alberto and Primo in our conversations (that would've required months of Mike-Leigh-type character research), but just drew on ourselves, our own experiences of bullying – him at boarding school, me in the army – our attitudes to our Jewishness (both non-practising), and our home lives; his with wife and kids, mine with

Greg. The warmth of these talks helped to counter the brutality of the guards.

Tonight I think I started to grasp something important about Primo's survival in Auschwitz.

There was an unintentionally comic aspect to this improvisation. Since much of it was in the dark, Richard couldn't see, grew bored, and called it off early. Everyone drank shots of the Polish vodka we brought back from Kraków, while I secretly celebrated the fact that 'Night' was the last of these impros.

Thursday 12th August 2004

In the afternoon, a survivor comes to talk to us. Trude Levi. No relation to Primo, but like him a secular Jew. Aged 80, born in Hungary, part of the last big round-up and deportation of Jews, the Hungarian Jews, in 1944 when she was aged 20. After being held briefly in Auschwitz, she was transferred to a slave labour camp, Hessisch-Lichtenau, attached to Buchenwald in Germany.

She speaks for about an hour and a half: eloquently, urgently, needing to get every detail right, but fast, fast, fast, the story streaming out of her. She is possessed both by quiet anger and special composure. Her body is immensely still – the only movement being one hand rubbing the other wrist. I feel tearful throughout. Mainly because of the terrible authenticity of her account, but also because it keeps occurring to me that she's the same generation as Mom, yet her mind is so bright, so clear. Her body is quite frail – white-haired, small, using a stick – but her spirit is very tough, surprisingly humorous, keenly focused.

When she and others were rounded up and put on the transport, she says they'd heard the horror stories of what lay ahead, but didn't believe them. 'Our imaginations didn't go that far.' Later, when it was all over, she went to live in Durban, South Africa. One day she was giving a talk to a Jewish group, when a woman said, 'I'm sure you suffered, my dear, but I'm also sure

you're exaggerating.' This woman's imagination didn't go that
far. But it so shocked Trude that she stopped talking publicly
about her experiences for several years.

(I recall, with some unease, that the same word, 'exaggerating', came up in our discussion about Josef Perl.)

Trude had another fright in South Africa, and tells us the
story:

While in Hessisch-Lichtenau, she was detailed to dig a grave
for the dog of the Commandant, Schaefer. He was a relatively
un-sadistic, strictly-by-the-rules man who personally supervised
the daily distribution of bread so that there was no cheating.
Digging the dog's grave was hard work – the soil was frozen.
At the end, Schaefer surprised Trude by thanking her. And
from then on, he would greet her in the camp – 'I'd become a
face, not just a number.' Later, when there was a selection, and
a group of prisoners – including Trude – were being sent back
to Auschwitz, the numbers turned out to be incorrect: 208 had
been chosen, yet the paperwork only required 206. Schaefer
took Trude and one other out of the group. The rest ended up
perishing in Auschwitz. 'I think he was driven more by his
devotion to bureaucracy than to me,' Trude tells us, with that
unexpected twinkle. Years later, in the early '50s, she was
staying at a guest farm in Natal, owned by friends. They were
in the dining room one evening when a new group of guests
arrived – it was Schaefer and his family. Trude began to shake.
She told her friends, who asked Schaefer to leave. 'Why didn't
I denounce him to the authorities?' she says to us; 'I'm not sure.
It would've made no difference – South Africa was full of Nazis
in those days – and he had saved my life, in a way.'

We all sit hushed and motionless during her accounts. From
time to time, she says, 'I have documentation' – as if still
defying that woman who doubted her in Durban – and at the
end she brings out a sheaf of papers: photocopies of the
Hessisch-Lichtenau records and other material. Perhaps the
most disturbing thing we learn from her today is that the

Hungarian deportation was so late in the war, and so frantic, that the SS couldn't kill them fast enough. They had to cut down the time in the gas chamber, from 20 minutes to 12. This meant some people weren't fully dead at the end, especially children, whose parents had held them close during the gassing. So they went into the ovens alive.

As we're winding up – and I can't recall the context – Trude tells us that in 1979, her son Ilan, a geneticist, committed suicide. The group goes even quieter than before. *After everything else she's been through.* She continues: 'This is not uncommon among survivors. Our children sometimes have problems. Are we bad parents? Difficult to trust? Are we emotionally damaged? I don't know.'

She's told us this news in the same calm way as she's told all her nightmarish stories. She's driven to reveal everything that's happened to her – she's published two books about her life – yet she will not permit herself any self-pity. She's way beyond grief. I stare at her. A bad parent? Difficult to trust? That seems unlikely. I instinctively trust her. She strikes me as naturally good.

But I'm being naive. She may look like everyone's favourite granny, but first and foremost she's a Holocaust survivor. We've barely scratched the surface of what she's been through, what she's known.

When I get home this evening, I feel tired and depressed. What's that line Macbeth says? I look it up: 'I have supped full with horrors.'

Friday 13th August 2004

Last day of the workshop.

An excellent morning. We're all very inspired and moved by Trude. Richard says, 'Trude *is* Primo. She's shown how to portray him. Full of experience on the inside, terrible experience, but completely composed on the outside. Did you notice

how still she was! There's something so special, so particular
about that stillness. It's not someone who's just survived an
ordinary tragedy, or even an ordinary disaster, it's someone
who's survived the Holocaust.'

We try another selection of short Testimonies, in the style of
Trude: refining every movement, every emotion, aiming for
complete stillness and simplicity, yet filled from within. It's
difficult to achieve, but when it works – when I see it happen
in the others – it's riveting. Actually, it's like good film acting:
the mask-like face, with everything happening out of sight, yet
shining through.

Although this is one of our best sessions, the curse of Friday
the 13th still strikes in the afternoon. We do our final reading
of *Primo* – the others sharing the text again, me just listening.
Our composer, Jonathan Goldstein, is present, along with a
cellist from the National. We've decided the music should sound
Italian rather than Jewish: Primo's land was in his soul rather
than his race. At present Jonathan has only composed rough
sketches for the cues indicated in the text. Richard also invites
him to try others whenever he feels it's appropriate. This surprises me. Whereas all our work over the past fortnight has
been about precision, about earning the right to serve up this
difficult material, now there's an element of busking in the
room. And we're talking about an important element. In a play
for one voice, any music becomes the second. Inevitably, and
through no fault of Jonathan's, some of it sounds wrong, and
happens in the wrong places. It stops me from being able to
hear the text clearly, and ends up confusing me rather badly.

It reminds me of that reading of *I.D.* we did here at the
Studio, when we'd miscast one of the actors. To a playwright
as inexperienced as I am, it was muddling. I ended up losing
confidence in the character itself, and subsequently tried a
draft where I cut it completely. In the same way, today's
reading has left me wondering whether we should consider
cutting the music. Or is the cello just the wrong instrument?

When I wrote the script I rather carelessly put in stage directions like 'A cello plays', mostly as a way of distinguishing this music – moments of underscoring and scene change – from the other kind, the little Auschwitz band (which will be done on appropriate instruments and pre-recorded). But both Jonathan and Richard feel a cello is right. It creates a sound closest to the human voice, apparently. My worry is that its natural tone is solemn and mournful; it has an ache to it, a sob, all of which will be disastrous for us. Jonathan reassures me that it's versatile. This is doubly important since Richard wants the cello not to just play music, but to create other sound effects too: the rhythm of the train, the dripping tap, the wind.

I resolve to discuss it with Richard. In the case of *I.D.* I reprieved the character I'd cut and put it back in the play, and thank God I did. So I've learned not to let these readings unleash rash decisions.

In the evening, Richard and I take the actors to a thank-you dinner at Metrogusto. They've been a terrific group, and I've learned a lot from watching them perform the testimony pieces. We've been through a lot together: the punishment exercises, the visits from the survivors, and all the other harrowing material we've heard, watched and read. Although the actors were properly paid by the Studio, it still feels like they were engaged in a selfless and generous act: helping me to prepare for the next part of the journey. I wish they could come along. And, as Richard says tonight, 'How are we going to play Fourball?'

Observing Richard tonight, observing how much people enjoy his company, and how funny he is, I'm struck by the fact that he's markedly different when he directs. In fact, maybe it's because of his other career, in Comedy, in what telly people call Light Ent., that makes him rather solemn and severe as a director. 'Victor Meldrew without the laughs,' I complained to Greg after one of the punishment exercises. Greg replied, 'You're doing a play about Auschwitz, and you want your

director to make you laugh?!' I suppose the truth of it is that
Richard and I have been friends for so long that he can please
or upset me in a flash, like only Greg or family can. I'm sure
it's the same for him.

Choosing a friend is not unlike choosing a partner. So what
draws me to Richard? His humour, his generosity, his passion
for human rights. He has a lie-detector built into him, he can
sniff out melodrama at fifty paces, he refuses to trade in
clichés. And there's something we share: we both feel we're
social outsiders. He's from a working-class family in Greenock,
I'm from a business family in Cape Town. Neither of us was
destined to become an actor or a director or a writer in the
heart of London; neither of us was destined to work at the
National Theatre of Great Britain.

Luckily, I remember to thank him for the workshop tonight.
He's put an enormous amount of preparation and care into it,
and I almost forgot to acknowledge it. That's another aspect of
being best friends: you can take one another for granted, you
can forget to say thanks.

Part Four

Rehearsing Primo

Monday 16th August 2004

In thirty-five years as an actor I've never had a stranger first day of rehearsals.

I walked into Rehearsal Room 3 at the National – and stopped in my tracks. I was here to do a one-man show, but the room was filled with people. It was explained to me that all new shows here start with a 'meet 'n' greet', so about thirty representatives of different departments were present. Nick H. made a speech, saying how proud the National was to be presenting this show, and thanking us for bringing it to them. (I pinched myself, remembering the long journey to reach this point.) Richard replied: 'I want to say hello to you all, on behalf of myself and the acting company' – getting a big laugh. I was invited to speak, but I just smiled and shook my head, knowing if I opened my mouth I'd get emotional. Then everyone left. And Richard and I were suddenly on our own, gazing slowly round the big empty space.

Then our stage management team returned, and they outnumbered us. Ernie Hall (stage manager), Angie Bissett (deputy stage manager), Thomas Vowles (assistant stage manager).

They'd already done a mark-up of our set on the floor, erected flats to create the back wall and the doorway, and placed my co-star – the wooden chair – in the middle of the room. We now selected photos from our Auschwitz trip to stick on the walls, as well the map of Oświęcim showing the lay-out of town and camps, and also various images which Richard had brought back from his research trip to the Washington Holocaust Museum in April. We requested two more maps: of Italy (to locate key places like Turin, Fossoli, Fossano), and of Europe (to trace the train journey and the location of Auschwitz). Angie immediately zipped off to find these. The team are going to be somewhat under-employed on this particular show, and I suspect anything we want will arrive with startling speed.

Rehearsal Room 3 has no windows, and this worries me. Natural light is important in rehearsal rooms (it's why the RSC had to abandon the underground ones at the Barbican and move to Clapham); it's important in any place where you're going to be spending day after day, week after week.

Richard said to be patient. If ever a show could be rehearsed without natural light it's this one.

We began. Me reading the first section, us both checking we understood everything, and making occasional cuts. Richard and I sat on chairs in a corner of the room, with Thomas next to us; he'll be 'on the book' for the next five weeks, following in the script, noting changes, and prompting. He's young, with cropped brown hair, a cheerful spirit, a Somerset accent.

Richard was merciless with me from the start: 'No, it needs to be more open . . . no, colour it less . . . be careful of that storyteller tone . . . I've got to believe these things happened to *you*.' Tough going, but he was right, and it soon started to sound better. Apart from the lunch break (when I noticed my hand was shaking and couldn't easily lift a forkful of peas to my mouth) we spent about five hours just on the first two pages, inching through them, word by word, often cross-checking with *If This Is A Man* or the Angier and Thomson biographies.

Drove home like a zombie. Greg's away for the week, visiting his parents in the Lake District, and the timing of his absence couldn't be worse. Went to bed at 10pm, setting the alarm for 6am, to do several hours of line-learning before work.

Tuesday 17th August 2004

Richard is being very co-operative about arranging rehearsal times so that I can continue seeing Marietta, my therapist, throughout this period. Normally I have to break off when I do a new show. But Marietta was fairly insistent – in a way that she isn't usually – that I keep up our sessions during *Primo*. She and I both know this is going to be make or break in terms of The Fear.

Marietta and I meet in an upstairs room at Edward House in Lisson Grove, next door to the clinic where I was treated in 1996 – then called Charter Nightingale, and then, briefly, Florence Nightingale, and now Capio Nightingale. Marietta is about my age, blonde, sexy (only a gay man is allowed to say that about his therapist), and Czech.

Today's session came as a big relief, offloading a lot of complicated stuff from the last fortnight: the Auschwitz exercises from the workshop, and the visit to the place itself. I did two drawings: one of me as a tiny figure being threatened by the German guards in the improvisations, and the second of me as a shadowy figure against the dark stained wall of the actual gas chamber. Marietta encouraged me, as she has before, to work out exactly what I want from *Primo*, so that the success or failure of it can be on my terms. Not critics, not audiences. What do I want from *Primo*? I still have difficulty answering this. Surely theatre is a public not private practice?

Back at the National, we continued our meticulous text-work, Richard being a little gentler today. A crucial decision was taken. When other characters appear in the story – like, say, Alex the Kapo, or Schmulek the patient in Ka-Be – I should act them only as well as Primo might; ie. act them like a non-actor. In most other one-man shows, these other characters allow the narrator to portray a gallery of other people, and it's why this form of theatre is often described as a 'tour de force'. We'll be depriving ourselves of this, as well as greatly reducing the opportunities for variations of tone, colour and pace. But of course that's precisely why Richard has proposed it. He wants the audience to believe that the person up on the stage has personally experienced Auschwitz – me in a way, not Primo – and they won't if they see an actor showing off. I agree with him – in principle. In reality, I don't know what it'll feel like.

Today we also began to watch *Shoah*, Claude Lanzmann's documentary which inspired me to adapt *If This Is A Man* as a testimony rather than a conventional play. The film lasts eight hours, so we'll proceed in segments. I was very struck by one of the survivors towards the beginning: he has a strange smile on his face, very vulnerable, very frightened – it's a slave's smile. Lanzmann asks him about it. He replies that sometimes you smile, sometimes you cry. Quite soon he's crying – recalling how he had to unload his own wife and daughter from a van used for gassing.

We're having considerable difficulty finding film of Primo himself – I'm eager to see him now, hear him talk. Yet the BBC documentary about him which we've got, *The Memory of the Offence*, made in 1992, only shows him in one long shot at the end, walking along a colonnade of pillars, and you never hear his voice. He appears briefly, incredibly briefly – for about 15 seconds – in the Holocaust episode of *The World At War* series, and most of this is taken up with him asking the interviewer whether his English is correct for 'cattle truck'. He's un-bearded, dark-haired, youngish. I suppose he wasn't yet that famous when it was made – early '70s? – or maybe they didn't fully realise who they were talking to. What a waste. But surely he was properly interviewed on television later on? Stage manager Ernie is looking into it, trawling the internet for clues, and if anyone can crack this, Ernie can.

When I left at the end of the day, one of the stage door-keepers – the wry-smiling, smokey-voiced Linda Tolhurst – gave me two letters from the 'S' pigeonhole. They startled me. Both were from the Jewish community, and both were hostile – angry that the first two previews of *Primo* are on the 24th and 25th of September. This is the eve and day of Yom Kippur, the holiest Jewish day of the year, the Day of Atonement, a day of fasting, of remembering the dead. One of the letters was a week old, and had been copied to Nick H., so he'd already replied on my behalf, saying that the scheduling was entirely the National's responsibility, and that – as a secular Jew – he wasn't aware of the date of Yom Kippur, and anyway why couldn't a non-Jewish audience come on that day? This evening I replied to the other one in similar fashion, stating that I was also a secular Jew, but far more importantly so was Primo Levi. I used his searing quote again: 'There was Auschwitz, therefore God cannot exist.'

But I hope there isn't going to be trouble over this.

Wednesday 18th August 2004

We decide to try staging the first three sections. If we don't start getting it onto its feet now, and wait till we text-work the whole script, we'll be stuck in our chairs for weeks to come.

'First question,' I say as I stand.

'Ye-e-es?' Richard says slowly, as though warning me not to start trouble already.

'Do I look at you as I talk?'

'How d'you mean?'

'Well, in performance, I'm going to look at the audience – look them straight in the eye.'

'Absolutely.'

'Well, you and Thomas are my audience for now, and Thomas has his head in the book, so that just leaves you. Do I look at you as I talk?'

'Oh I see what you mean. Yes, I'm not sure about that. I directed Chris Fulford in some monologues at the Court, and he looked me in the eye as we rehearsed. Must say it was quite exhausting.'

'Five weeks of it ahead.'

'Hmn. Probably not, then.'

'Probably not. I'll talk to the walls for now.'

'You do that.'

'There we go – first problem solved.'

I've never had any stage pictures in my head for *Primo*, which is unusual for me. I just imagined it would be played as a very stark, Beckett-like monologue, and perhaps I wouldn't move at all. So it comes as a relief to discover that Richard is brimming with ideas. Movement is possible, though it has to be minimalist, and carefully choreographed. Particularly exciting is the discovery that each section can have a different *colour* of movement. In the first, 'The Journey', which is retrospective, I can be Primo in post-war mode: relaxed, easy, hands in pockets, as if addressing a univesity audience, say. In the second, 'The Platform', which is now in the present tense, stillness rules and each move counts: one step forward means I've climbed off the train, one to the side means I'm selected to live, another forward and I'm loaded onto the lorry. For the next, 'The First Twenty-four Hours', everything becomes more naturalistic: the set is the big empty room into which we're herded, and the opening at the back is the doorway through which various people arrive – the SS man, the manic barbers – and then, as the day progresses and Primo is transferred from place to place, I move all over the stage, which Richard says he might light in separate areas.

With only one man in an open space, the smallest gesture can become powerful. When the train stops, and Primo says, 'We waited for what would happen', just taking my hands out of my pockets adds to the tension. When the prisoners are stripped, folding my hands over my crotch becomes an image for nakedness – which we can use repeatedly throughout the show.

Really felt very encouraged by the end of the afternoon. Richard was an inspiring presence all day, though also surprisingly dictatorial. I know I asked him to push me, yet I was nevertheless expecting us to work together as equals. But he's of the school of directors (and they're often very good teachers) who have a Theory of Acting, a strict, singular view of the craft, and therefore need to exert total control in the rehearsal room. Other directors tend to be freer, proceeding through discussion and negotiation, even if they retain the right to have the last say. Greg always jokes that directing is tyranny disguised as democracy. Well, Richard doesn't really bother with the disguise. This almost led to our first falling out . . .

When rehearsals were over, I went up to the Wardrobe Department with Hildegard and Hattie Barsby (Costume Supervisor) to find some rehearsal clothes, or maybe even the real thing. Primo will be wearing shirt, tie, short-sleeved cardigan, trousers and neat polished shoes. The latter are crucial because of all the text about shoes: in Auschwitz, these were wooden soled or complete clogs, and extremely painful, often leading in quick succession to sores, swelling, slowness of movement, punishment, death.

Up in the fitting room, the atmosphere was very relaxed. We had glasses of wine, and were browsing through the clothes and shoes selected as possibilities by Hildegard and Hattie ('You two sound like a German cabaret act,' I observed). Most of the shirts were blue. I said white might be better, because I always sweat on stage, and blue would show the damp patches. 'Richard has said I'm not allowed to sweat in this show,' I told them; 'And although I've conveyed the message to my sweat glands, I'm not sure they're going to obey Bossy Boots quite like the rest of us.'

We were laughing about this when he came in.

He said he didn't expect wine to be flowing at a costume fitting. We looked at him in puzzlement, since it wasn't the wine but he who was out of place. It's very unusual for a director to attend fittings, or even a casual viewing like this. The director will have discussed 'the look' beforehand of course, but then he or she normally waits to see what the designer and actor come up with – which can always be changed or adjusted. I'm very particular about the appearance of my characters, and since I'm regarded as having a fairly decent visual sense, designers tend to respect this, and we work together happily, feeding off one another's ideas.

So it came as a surprise when it was not even a designer but a director striding round the room, selecting the costume: 'This . . . this . . . this.' It turned out he'd already requested certain items for me to try on: a Fair Isle sweater and brogues.

'I thought Primo was from Turin,' I commented; 'Now I find he's from Edinburgh.'

This was said lightly. Hildegard and Hattie laughed. Richard didn't. He became increasingly impatient with my suggestions. I thought a slip-on shoe would be very Italian. No – he wanted lace-ups. I thought a sober tie was required, indicating a modest dresser, without vanity. No – he wanted a bright, patterned tie.

Since nothing in the room was immediately suitable, Hildegard and Hattie resolved to search further, maybe do some shopping, show us further options. Also, since Richard and I are going on a research trip to Turin in a couple of weeks, it would be ideal if we could find some of the costume there.

'I'm sure we'll all know when we see the right thing,' I said.

'Trouble is, we'll all know differently,' muttered Richard.

I stared at him in amazement. Was he really bemoaning the democracy of modern-day theatre?

I came close to losing my temper several times – as you only can with someone close to you. I wanted to say: 'I'm not some kid straight from drama school working at the Court, y'know, I don't need you to choose my fucking costume for me.'

I'm glad I didn't though, glad I kept my cool, particularly since it was in front of Hildegard and Hattie. Richard and I have been working together well on this. It would've been a shame to let a bit of end-of-day tiredness spoil things.

In a one-man show the costume is vitally important, obviously, but it will have to feel right for all of us – Hildegard, Richard and me – and that will probably mean some compromises. However, these will not extend to me wearing a Fair Isle sweater and brogues.

Thursday 19th August 2004

After we finished blocking 'The First Twenty-four Hours', Richard suggested running the first three sections. I said I doubted if I'd remember all the moves (sometimes it's just a turn of the head, a point of the finger) and we might have to stop. He said that was fine. I took a deep breath. Fifteen minutes later I finished, having got through it all without stopping, and almost word perfect. Richard was delighted – 'Tony, what are we going to do for the next four weeks?!' I must say I was pleased, relieved, and encouraged. A map, a geography, for the piece is emerging, and it feels exciting.

Friday 20th August 2004

Woke exhausted. Could hardly get out of bed. Luckily today was short. Richard had to fly up to Scotland – he's presenting one of the television awards at the Edinburgh Festival – and left mid-afternoon. After he'd gone, I ran the lines of the first fifteen pages (the first half) with ASM Thomas, and found I'm pretty much word-perfect. Then Ernie joined us, and we had a drink together. Normally actors and stage management don't socialise much, and tend to keep to their own groups – but if that happens on *Primo* I'm gong to end up rather lonely. So the breaking down of this barrier is another aspect of this job that's unusual, and good. Ernie has grey hair, little specs, and is a very comforting presence; he puts me in mind of Primo's description of Lorenzo, in that he has a 'natural and plain manner of being good'. Ernie's been at the National for yonks (since 1974). We talk about Michael Bryant. In the production of *Arturo Ui* that I did here, Michael played the hammy old actor who teaches Ui (Hitler) his range of histrionic gestures. It was the best scene in the show, and we got on famously. Throughout the National, Michael is still much loved, much remembered. Ernie's favourite story is of the tech for *Wind in the Willows*, in which Michael played Badger and Richard Briers was Rattie. In one section, Briers had to repeatedly cross the set in a diagonal line. Each time he reached centre stage he skirted round it, then continued. Eventually Nick H., who was directing, asked him what he was doing.

Briers: I'm avoiding Michael Bryant.

Nick H.: But he's not there.

Briers: No, but he will be.

Back at home, I was surprised to see Greg's car parked outside. He wasn't due back till late tonight. Our reunion was joyous, as it always is. Every goodbye hurts, every hello delights. I'm incomplete without him.

Sunday 22nd August 2004

Dear God. Having weathered those angry letters about *Primo*'s first performances falling on Yom Kippur, I got another fright this morning. Leafing through the Culture section of the Sunday Times, I found a big article about the *Churchill* film with several photos of me as Hitler. Since I hadn't heard anything about the film recently (and wasn't available to go to the cast and crew screening), I glanced to the credits at the end of the article, to see when it was opening. September 24th. Yom Kippur.

So – on Yom Kippur this year I'm going to be playing both Primo Levi and Adolf Hitler.

Greg says I could get lynched.

Tuesday 24th August 2004

Four weeks to go.

Having done the text-work and blocking on sections 4, 5, 6 – 'On the Bottom', 'Ka-Be', 'A Good Day' – we ran that sequence. Much tougher than the first lot, and lasted twice as long: half an hour. I was also struck by the strain of a one-man show, or maybe just *this* one-man show, the relentlessness of it – me just talking, talking, talking – something hypnotic, but in a potentially boring sense. Isn't Richard's insistence on me never colouring the lines leading to a same-iness? Or is it just a phase we're going through? Don't know, we'll see. Ended the day, half-alarmed, half-encouraged. What have I created for myself here? I'm particularly worried that we're not putting in enough water-stops (during the blackouts I'll drink from a glass hidden in the side wall). What if my dry-mouth affliction strikes?

Unfortunately Marietta is away this week. I need to talk to her.

Back at home, discussing it with Greg, I told him that to-day's little run reminded me of doing the Iago soliloquies during our Japanese tour. The audiences there love Shakespeare, and their focus is phenomenal. They sit for three-and-a-half hours, rapt and silent. Too silent for Iago. He needs interaction, and some laughter. The audience are one of his victims: he seduces them, tells them everything, they delight in the complicity, and then end up horrified by the consequences. But our Japanese audiences, hampered by the simultaneous translation and an almost over-respectful attitude to the RSC, never quite went on this journey with Iago. Their silence became eerie. I was left with the same sensation as this afternoon: the sound of my own voice talking, talking, talking. No-one else present. Just me and my demons.

'What if The Fear happens during *Primo*?' I asked Greg.

'As I've said before, it won't – *Primo* is too important.'

'Oh what does that mean?!' I cried; 'Why wasn't Iago important? Or Domitian?'

'They were,' he replied calmly; 'But not as important as this.'

'Oh bollocks,' I said, walking away, praying he's right.

In the evening we watched a documentary on David Beresford's battle with Parkinson's. I've always admired Beresford – South African correspondent for the Guardian – and admired him even more tonight. But the brain surgery was difficult to watch. He has to be conscious throughout, with his head held motionless in a metal clamp. A whole team of people surround him, working on different parts of his body: the surgeon and assistants at his head, nurses flexing his hands or moving his legs to keep him active during the long ordeal (thirteen hours). In a different context, these could be torturers. Yet this was to help him, to heal him. We are so bloody vulnerable.

Wednesday 25th August 2004

A rough night of bad dreams and sleeplessness. At 6am, I was lying in bed feeling exhausted and anxious – we run the first half today – when Greg said he had to be out early, and got up. I had just started to doze again when I became aware of him climbing back under the covers. He urgently whispered, 'They're here!' I said, 'Who?' Realised there was torch light coming up the stairs. I began to weep: 'I haven't slept all night, and I don't know what's going on!' Greg comforted me – except he was weird – hair wet on one side, a leering smile. 'Is this a dream?' I sobbed; 'It is, isn't it . . . ?'

I woke, gasping, realising that I hadn't been awake before – at 6 – I'd just been going from one evil dream to another, except the last masqueraded as reality. Greg, the real Greg, who had never got up, moved over and hugged me. I wept – for real, this time.

After all this, I was surprisingly concentrated and relaxed at rehearsals. When it came to the run of the first half, I said to Richard, 'I'm going to tell everyone to ignore your Royal Court reputation – you're just an old reppy director who makes his cast run half the bloody play in the second bloody week!' He laughed merrily.

The run was weird, weirder than anything I've ever done. Felt I was floating in space, electrified space, all alone. Sometimes I felt good, sometimes nervous, sometimes emotional – my voice on the edge of breaking – and sometimes, most alarmingly, I didn't know what came next. Not the lines (I only dried twice) but the sequence of the story itself, which is episodic. It happened on two occasions, and although I remembered in time, I got two bad frights. God knows what it'll be like to do the whole piece. The run lasted 52 minutes, which is probably too long. Richard was pleased by it. I was shell-shocked. Couldn't meet his eye for a while. Felt a kind of Primo Levi shame. Whether for the humiliations Primo endures, or for my inadequacy portraying them, I'm not sure.

Thursday 26th August 2004

Despite a sleeping pill, my night was awful once more. Awake from 3 to 5, and then a string of little nightmares, which woke me again and again. What's going on in my head? What's lodging there? Don't know. Just get out!

At rehearsals, as a result of yesterday's run, Richard asked me to do the opening sequence over and over, so that it can become relaxed, easy, second nature, and not feel like the start of a marathon. Only a fellow actor would understand this somehow, picturing what it would be like to wait in the wings before a one-man show, and be able to think of this solution.

The gentleness was back in Richard today, the gentleness which I thought would characterise him as a director, and which doesn't really. But something has relaxed in him because of yesterday's run. I guess he realised, like I did, that this can work. It's becoming more of a *production* than either of us probably anticipated. Auschwitz is gradually appearing on-stage, if only in the air, and Richard hasn't even started adding music and lights. I think the end result is going to be as much about his work as mine. So he's been nervous too. And I've been forgetting that. Which is stupid of me. I live with a director – I know what they go through.

After rehearsals, the costume supervisor Hattie and I went to try and find Primo's shoes. She thought Harrods might have the best selection. We looked at a pair that seemed right (smart, but delicate, modest) and were a good colour (a reddish brown, which will show well on the lead floor), and, best of all, they were Italian. But they were slip-ons. I said Richard felt strongly that they should be lace-ups, which are more conservative. As I tried the shoes on, I was repeatedly saying things like, 'But he said . . . well he wants . . . ', until the assistant interrupted, and said, 'I'm sorry, are these not for you?' Afterwards, Hattie and I couldn't stop laughing at the idea that I was the servant – a footman, I suppose – of someone so posh they don't shop for their own shoes.

Anyway, we bought the Harrods shoes (which can be returned), and then traipsed over to Bond Street, and found another pair, which weren't as good but were lace-ups, and bought them too (they can also be returned).

I braced myself for a fight in the morning.

Friday 27th August 2004

To my surprise, Richard instantly said the slip-ons were better: perfect, in fact.

So – good – at least I've got Primo's feet now.

I couldn't refrain from lightly gloating: 'You see, I said we'd all know when something was right.'

Richard said the trouble was we were both just following our instincts about Primo's way of dressing, and although we had some photographs as guidlines, these tended to be rather formal: Primo had always spruced himself up for the camera. We needed to know what he looked like in ordinary life. Richard said he would e-mail some friends in Italy; they knew a man who had worked with Primo at Einaudi.

We had a short day (Richard flying to Scotland again for a meeting about a future project) and relatively unpressured, since it was mostly text-work. But we did start staging 'A Chemistry Exam' and found that the chair can play Dr Pann- witz, the German chemist who tests Primo's knowledge, decid- ing whether he's qualified to work in the lab. Doing the scene facing the chair feels very strong. The strength of simplicity, I suppose. If you've got nothing on stage, everything resonates. In the past, I've always said of auditions, 'It's ridiculous, playing speeches into the middle distance or to a chair!' – but I never will again. In this show, when I get to 'A Chemistry Exam', it's going to be such a relief to talk to a chair.

Saturday 28th August 2004

Although this is a day off, it's back to the National: Greg and I went to the matinee of Alan Bennett's *The History Boys*. It was as good as everyone says; a play with a big heart, full of warmth and wisdom. The boys were terrific, Frankie de la Tour on top form, and Richard Griffiths superb. He does very impressive internalised acting (a good lesson for *Primo*), so much so that at one point it took a moment to realise he'd come out of character and stopped the show to berate someone in the front row whose mobile had gone off six times. As the disgraced man fled the auditorium, the audience applauded. I cheered. (I hate our lack of etiquette with mobile phones; in Japan, they're auto-

matically banned on trains and the tube, in restaurants, theatres
and cinemas.) And then, completely unruffled, Griffiths just
slipped back into the scene.

As we left, we caught sight of a *Primo* poster, which shows
me lifting specs, and is a copy of a famous photo of the man
himself. There are very few of these posters about – for a special
reason. The show has sold out on the mailing list. The National
scheduled thirty performances in the end, but as our producer
Pádraig said to me, 'I think we may have underestimated the
public interest in this.' The box office is now besieged by angry
customers who can't buy tickets (apparently someone wrote, 'I
was in Auschwitz, but can't get into *Primo*!'), and so the National
is in the unusual position of trying to downplay the whole event.
They're only putting up a limited number of posters, and not
taking out any newspaper ads. I understand the logic behind
this, yet feel slightly bereft. It feels as though *Primo* doesn't
quite live in this building.

The National is on a phenomenal run of success at the
moment – playing to something like 90% on every show in
every auditorium, and critically lauded to the skies, with hit
following hit. I congratulated Nick H. on this the other day in
the canteen, where he's to be found every single lunchtime,
unlike some previous Artistic Directors (the first time I worked
here in 1982 on *True West*, I never saw Peter Hall once, I never
met him). Nick said, 'Yes it's great, but of course you think:
When will it end?' I thought: Not with us, I hope.

Sunday 29th August 2004

During my line-learning session this morning, I suddenly tried
doing the whole piece. Found that I knew it. All of it. God.
What a marathon though. It lasted 1 hour 45 minutes, which
means there's still at least 15 minutes to be cut.

Later I rang Mom – for the first time in ages. It's awful, but
I keep putting it off, thinking it doesn't matter if I ring or not,

she doesn't really notice. Today she certainly seemed vaguer than before. Wasn't surprised and delighted by my call; normally she begins with 'How nice to hear your voice!' This time it was as if we'd spoken yesterday – I suppose she has no way of knowing we didn't. Nor did she seem to have any awareness that I'm bringing *Primo* home in January, although I've told her, and the family keep telling her. Also, she normally asks after Greg, and I'm always impressed that she effortlessly remembers his name. This time she just sent regards to 'everyone there'.

Monday 30th August 2004

Bank holiday. Another day off. Which was unnerving. (Would paying overtime for the *Primo* company have crippled the National?) Went through all the lines again. Got the time down to 1 hour 40 minutes.

After lunch, Greg took me to the workshop of the Little Angel Theatre down an Islington lane, where the puppets are being made for his production of *Venus and Adonis* – inspired by him seeing Bunraku in Japan. Despite the bank holiday, all the craftsmen were there, working away. It didn't seem like work; there was a serenity, a contentment among them all, as though they were just indulging their favourite hobby. I envied them. Acting hasn't felt like that for a long time. Lyndie Wright, a South African who founded the place with her late husband John, is a warm maternal character. With these gentle people creating beautiful objects, and the sunshine streaming through the skylight, there was a tranquility here – the exact opposite of Auschwitz somehow – which made me want to switch jobs instantly, and volunteer my services as a painter.

Tuesday 31st August 2004

Three weeks to go.

Richard's Italian friends have contacted the man who used to work at Einaudi, Ernesto Ferrero, and he's confirmed that Primo was a very sober dresser: 'like a professor at a provincial university' is his evocative description.

In rehearsals we blocked sections 7, 8, 9 – 'A Chemistry Exam', 'Lorenzo', 'Selekcja' – and again the solutions of staging each episode were both easy and exciting.

We got to one of the passionate moments: Primo saying 'I judge you' after the Kapo Alex has wiped a dirty hand on his shoulder. There are only about three or four of similar moments in the whole piece, moments charged with emotion, and when I practise these particular lines at home I always get upset. Which seems valid. The calm rational scientist is suddenly shaken by real feeling. But of course Richard pounced on it today: 'You were pressing a bit there, just let the thought do it, it's more chilling.' I wanted to answer, 'It's not about thought, it's about feeling', but held back. I'm often holding back in these rehearsals. Why? Partly because Richard's certainty is truly intimidating (I'm discovering something new about us: in a rehearsal room, I prefer questions, he prefers answers), but more importantly, I sense that his instinct for the part is better than my own. As a man, he is more Primo than I am; he's less emotional, more self-disciplined. Maybe I've been secretly – no, unconsciously – using him as a model for the role. Later we got to another of these passionate moments: when, after the Selection, Primo hears old Kuhn thanking God that he's been spared, and explodes – 'If I was God I would spit at Kuhn's prayer!' This time, Richard 'allowed' some emotion, although (and I laughed at this inwardly) he placed me very far upstage. Any further and I would have escaped captivity.

At home, an evening ritual has come into being. Greg and I work separately (him preparing *Venus and Adonis*, me writing my diary) while sipping at glasses of our namesake, G & T, then join together for soup at seven o'clock, watching the

Channel 4 News. Tonight the headlines were even more appalling than usual: 12 Nepalese hostages executed in Iraq, 16 Israelis
killed in 2 suicide bombings, 10 Russians killed by a Chechen
bomb in Moscow. All this in the context of 1 man struggling to
live in Auschwitz. At eight o'clock we have our main course,
which Greg makes these days (since I'm the working one), and
again this is eaten in front of the telly. Tonight there was a treat
on BBC2, the perfect antidote to all human foulness: a wildlife
programme – a new series on Australia. By 10 I'm getting
sluggish, and with a 6am rise ahead to learn lines, I go up to bed
and read for half an hour (currently a biography of John
Schlesinger, who directed *True West* and was a friend) before
going to sleep . . . nowadays with half a pill, to try and ward off
the nightmares . . .

Wednesday 1st September 2004

Fairly relaxed day. We blocked sections 10, 11, 12 – 'The Lab',
'The Last One', 'Final Days' – finding excellent shapes for
each of them, as before. And I contributed an idea today, my
first! When Charles and Primo have tipped Sómogyi's corpse
next to the common grave, and are paying respects, and the
Russians arrive, I suggested standing with my back to the
audience, and then swinging round to see our liberators. Even
as I write this, I'm aware it's more 'theatrical' than the other
movements in the piece, which are entirely Richard's, and
excellent I think. I'm actually enjoying being completely
directed in this show, probably for the first time ever. I just do
what I'm told.

It's a credit to our friendship that, in the context of these
rehearsals, where we spend all day locked endlessly in one
another's company, we still choose to spend our lunch hour
together rather than fleeing apart. We have a salad in the
canteen, then a walk along the Thames. Among the advantages

of working at the National is that a lunchtime stroll takes you
past one of London's most beautiful views. Stratford offers a
similar treat. The Barbican never did.

This afternoon our lighting designer, Paul Pyant, popped in.
He's extremely busy opening the new big Trevor Nunn
musical, *Woman in White*, but had a few hours to spare. I felt
touched that he wanted to catch up, wanted to see what we're
doing. He's a big, gentle, humorous man, nicknamed Polly, and
I warmed to him instantly.

We ran a few sections for him. My first audience. He was very
encouraging.

Thursday 2nd September 2004

I'm woken at about 3 by a nightmare. Can't remember the
details, but a phrase from the 'Selekcja' section kept recurring
. . . 'the *schlechte Seite* (bad side)' . . . which meant your card
had landed with those going to the gas chamber. I lie awake for
two hours, and as soon as I drop off, the string of little cruel
dreams starts up, disturbing my sleep repeatedly. In one, a hand
reaches forward and slaps my face, instantly waking me.

*I'm having trouble sleeping, so I dream of a hand slapping me
awake . . . ?! Who needs enemies when we've got the inside of our
own heads?*

Luckily Marietta is back, and we have one of our best sessions this morning. She presses me again on what I want from
Primo. What do I want? Me. Nothing to do with audiences or
critics, just my own needs.

I answer, rather lamely: 'I want to do justice to Primo Levi's
material . . . it's become very important now . . . I want to stop
The Fear fucking this one up.'

She says, 'So often you talk of your work in terms of fear,
frustration, disappointment – can't you do this one out of love?'

I go still, and listen attentively. It's very untypical for Marietta,
or any good therapist, to recommend a course of action; you

usually have to discover it for yourself.

And what an interesting word she used . . . love.

When, as a child or teenager, you sense a talent for any of the creative arts it's like an animal instinct at first, almost a sexual instinct – you're simply drawn to a particular object of desire, and probably can't even explain why. This transforms into infatuation: you can't think of it enough, you can't think of anything else. Next, it becomes unadulterated love. Then, if you're lucky enough to turn it into your job, it becomes the equivalent of a marriage or partnership. And then reality sets in . . . the cruelty and uncertainty of theatre, for example . . . and then, if you're not careful, it can turn into a bad marriage, a stale partnership: hard work, unsatisfying, unsettling, just there, always there. And that's exactly what's happened to me with acting. The love has gone out of it.

Marietta continues, 'If you care so much about Primo Levi, can't you create some kind of dialogue with him?'

'How do you mean?' I ask.

'I don't know. What might it be? A series of drawings maybe.'

I sit thinking, then say: 'When I was last at the National, it was as Stanley Spencer. He wrote letters to his dead wife, Hilda. He'd sort of killed her, by marrying someone else, but he loved her dearly, and wrote daily. Maybe I could do that. Write letters.'

'To Primo Levi?'

'Yes.'

'OK, good. But write them with love.'

I drive to work, inspired by this idea.

We finish blocking the last section, and then run 10, 11, and 12. It all feels strong. I think what the production is doing is creating a kind of dream, a bad dream . . . like the ones I'm having at the moment.

Tomorrow we're going to Turin for the weekend (Richard, me, and Greg). This doesn't sound as strange as saying, 'We're going to Auschwitz for the weekend', yet nevertheless holds a certain tension. The Levi family have said they can't meet us.

Renzo (Levi's son) would have been happy to, but unfortunately he's out of town. And Lucia (Levi's widow) would find
it too traumatic on her own. No word from Lisa (Levi's
daughter). After the blessing they bestowed on this project, I
was of course hoping to meet them, and to go to the apartment
at 75 Corso Re Umberto, where Primo lived for 64 out of the
67 years of his life, so it's disappointing, but acceptable. We
have to bear in mind they were distressed by the two British
biographies in 2002, and particularly by the material about his
death. (Out of respect, I've already said to Lyn Haill, who does
the programmes at the National, that we'll declare the date of
his death without saying how it happened.) Einaudi, Primo's
publishers, are laying on a big tour for us – Primo's school, his
university, and the paint factory where he worked as a chemist
after the war – and I feel sure there are many riches ahead.

Friday 3rd September 2004

Re-reading the end of Angier's biography on the plane to
Turin, I was in tears: her interpretation of that moment on
Saturday 11th April 1987 (*where I was then? . . . in Stratford . . .
playing Shylock . . . falling in love with Greg . . .*), at about 10.15
in the morning, when Primo leans over the balustrade looking
for Lucia – who's popped out to do some shopping – and then
falls. He lands on the lobby floor below; the same lobby that
he's crossed thousands and thousands of times, as a toddler, a
schoolboy, a university student, a man returning from Auschwitz, a writer, a chemist, a depressive . . .
    Later:

Grand Hotel Sitea, Via Carlo Alberto, Torino

Dear Primo,
    This is my first letter to you. Written on hotel stationery
in your hometown. I'll paste it in my diary when we get

back to London. Future letters will probably just be written straight into the diary. That's how this will work.

Driving from the airport into Turin, I was full of anti-
cipation to see your part of the world. It's curious. Unlike
any other Italian city I know. Whereas the others are so
open, so full of light and energy, here in Turin – even on
a bright hot afternoon like this – the feeling was rather restrained and sombre. It's partly the grey local stone, partly
the dull neo-classical architecture, partly the narrow streets,
which are constructed, curiously, on a grid system, so that
everywhere's very ordered, very straight – left-right, left-
right – and there's none of the sensuous tumble and sprawl
of most Italian places. Apparently in the winter it's also very
damp and foggy. Your people, the Turinese, are known as
'the cold fish' of Italy, or 'the British', and this isn't meant
as a compliment. Turin is not somewhere for a depressive.

As soon as we arrived at the hotel, we switched on
CNN. We'd already heard – back at Gatwick – that the
Chechnyan siege at the Russian school had been broken.
Despite Russian promises that force wouldn't be used,
when they heard explosive noises coming from the school,
they moved in, bullishly, clumsily, and hundreds of lives
have already been lost – hostages and captors, including a
lot of children. Modern-day terrorism is a savage thing.
At least in the Lager you had selections – 'a fraction of a
second', as you put it – when the SS decided who'd live or
die. Terrorism isn't so choosy. Terorrism makes Auschwitz
look civilised.

With love,
Tony.

Saturday 4th August 2004

In Stratford there's the Shakespeare tour, in Bath the Jane
Austen tour, in London the Dickens tour. Today, here in

Turin, Richard and I take the Primo Levi tour (while Greg sets off on a more conventional day of sightseeing).

Our guide is the Einaudi representative who made all this happen, our man in Turin, Roberto Gilodi. He's bespectacled, tall, dark, with a soft, ready laugh and a surprising accent, German – his first language. Italian is his second, English third. As we set off, he apologises for his car – which is a worn but rather sexy black '60s Fiat. (During the day, when people approach us with cameras, I keep thinking Turin is full of *One Foot in the Grave* fans, only to realise it's the car they're interested in.) Roberto says, 'We are going to start at the university, where Professor Chiantore will show us round the *Dipartimenti Chimici*, the Chemistry Faculty, and where Renzo might meet us also.'

I'm in the back seat. I lean forward: 'Sorry . . . Renzo as in Renzo Levi, Primo's son?'

'Yes,' says Roberto; 'He lectures there – in chemistry.'

'But . . . we thought he wasn't in Turin this weekend.'

'So did I. But he phoned me this morning. He's here. And he might come along.'

'Oh . . . right,' I say, suddenly feeling anxious. I'd reconciled myself to not meeting the family. Now I might. What will that feel like? I hope I can keep my emotions in check.

Primo's University
The *Dipartimenti Chimici* has a grand lobby, with a wide marble staircase. The head of the faculty, Professor Oscar Chiantore, takes us into the lecture room first: a steep bank of wooden seats, high ornate windows. Above the lecturer's platform is a giant periodic table, dedicated to Primo, and with a quote from him, which Roberto translates roughly as: 'Understanding the universe and matter and ourselves . . . therefore the periodic table of Mendeleyev was a poem.'

The labs are on the first floor. I lift my nose, scenting the air, remembering Primo's words when he enters the lab at Auschwitz: 'The smell makes me start back as if from the blow of a whip: the weak aromatic smell of organic chemistry laboratories. For a moment, the large semi-dark room at the university, my fourth year, the mild air of May in Italy comes back to me with brutal violence and immediately vanishes.' In the library, I notice that quite a few of the books are in English. 'It is the international language of Chemistry,' explains Professor Chiantore; 'Before the Second World War, it was German.' Richard and I stop in our tracks, and look at one another. Throughout rehearsals something has been puzzling us in the story: how on earth did Primo take an oral chemistry exam in German, a language he didn't speak? At last we understand.

As we're leaving, Professor Chiantore gives us a copy of Primo's final-year thesis, as well as a programme from the Primo Levi Celebration held here in 1997, the tenth anniversary of his death. There's a photo of the audience in the lecture room, with Lucia and Renzo on the front row. Renzo doesn't look much like his father; he has a rounder, heavier face.

It's good to see him at last, for he hasn't turned up here in person . . .

Primo's School
Liceo Classico Massimo D'Azeglio. Like the university, and like his publishers, this building is just a walk or bicycle ride away from Primo's home, Roberto tells us. Quite a lot of his life was spent within quite a small radius. The school was converted from a convent in 1866. It has austere shadowy corridors, with glass cases holding stuffed birds and animals.

We're taken into the study of the headmaster, Professor Franco Massaia. There's quite a crowd in here. Another professor – Flavio Sarni – who's just retired as head of English, several ladies who are on the staff and have kindly dug out Primo's school reports and photocopied them for us, and a journalist and photographer. Professor Sarni now proceeds to interview us about our interest in Primo Levi (hang on, aren't

we supposed to be asking the questions?), while Professor
Massaia whispers a translation to the journalist. When this is
over, the two professors tell us that Primo was a gifted pupil –
on his reports, he consistently gets *otto* for most subjects, and
dieci for *Condotta* (Good Behaviour) – but in his final year he
failed Written Italian. They laugh about this: was it because the
subject didn't interest him (Italy's involvement in the Spanish
Civil War) or just because the teacher was an idiot?

They both knew Primo in his later life. I ask whether it's
true that the Turinese are like the British, possessing great
reserve, and whether this was the case with Primo? Professor
Massaia grins – 'Oh yes, he was *molto* Turinese!' Professor
Sarni tells us about Primo's style as a public speaker: 'Very still,
very clear . . . to hear him speak was like reading his books . . .
almost geometric . . . connected to his inner soul.' (I see
Richard looking pleased: Professor Sarni has just given me
some good acting notes.)

They take us on a tour of the school, everyone else
following, chattering among themselves, the journalist jotting
notes, the photographer snapping away, and Professor Massaia
taking the opportunity of these perambulations to have a sly
fag, cupping it in his palm like a naughty kid. I feel I'm in a
procession from some Fellini film. (Turin used to have some of
the best film studios in Italy.) We go into the gymnasium, a
room Primo would have dreaded when he was actually at
school. (Like me, he wasn't sporty.) Apparently, he returned
here as an adult – in the mid '70s – to address the pupils (Renzo
was one of them then). Primo was concerned: it was the time
of the rise of Neo-Fascism in Europe, and schoolchildren were
being targeted. Primo later wrote that for the second time in
his life he found himself fighting Fascism. It was a fight he felt
he was losing, and this contributed to the crushing depressions
before his death.

Primo's Publishers

Einaudi. How that strange Italian name (pronounced Ay-now-dee) has resonated in my skull for the last two years. How like enemies they seemed. Now friends. And here we are, on a hot Saturday afternoon. Their office stands on the wide leafy avenue of Corso Re Umberto, just a few blocks from Primo's home. The building is closed today, but Roberto guides us through a side entrance, producing special keys, pressing codes and opening doors. A security man suddenly appears. He's armed. He takes us to an upper floor where Einaudi is located. He can't get the lights to work. Roberto leads us down the dark corridor and into a large dark room. Here he throws open the wooden shutters, and sunlight streams in. We're in the conference room.

Primo would have sat at this big round table; he was on the editorial committee for several years. Just a day or two before Primo died, Signor Einaudi himself visted his apartment and invited him to become President of the publishing house. Surrounding the table are bookcases filled with Einaudi's distinctive small white editions. On the wall, Roberto shows us a picture of Einaudi's logo – an ostrich – and invites us to guess why this creature was chosen. 'Well, it can't be because it sticks its head in the sand,' I say (while thinking it sometimes felt exactly like that during negotiations). Roberto gives his soft musical laugh: 'No! It's because Signor Einaudi used to say "Our souls can digest the hardest things in the world".'

Primo's Factory

Called SIVA, the paint factory is a twenty-minute drive out of the city. I picture Primo making this journey every morning. Was it with a sense of relief? His home life sounds oppressive: his aged mother Rina was very ill, yet ruled the roost (it was her home, after all) in competion with Lucia. However, I have to remind myself that this information is from the biographies, which have displeased the family, so maybe it's inaccurate.

For thirty years after the war, Primo worked long hours at
SIVA, first just as a chemist (using his skills to manufacture
different paints and varnishes), later as manager. In this capacity he had to go on foreign trips, Roberto tells us, and at one
reception in Germany a woman said to him, 'You speak our language very well – where did you learn it?' Without hesitation,
he replied, 'Auschwitz.' Now there's a conversation closer.

We reach SIVA. Primo's other life. A plain industrial complex. Closed now, and most of it in the process of demolition,
to make room for the new Turin–Milan–Lyon railway line. But
the blue iron gates still stand and one building with mustard-
coloured walls, which is going to become a Primo Levi museum.

Primo's Home
75 Corso Re Umberto. These are some more Italian words
which have been in my consciousness for a long time. In fact,
this address, rather like the gate at Auschwitz, has acquired
mythic status for me. I feel nervous as we approach, and heavy-
hearted. It's because of Primo's death. Whenever this subject
came up in the past I felt like a detective following clues, and
now I'm about to view the scene of the incident – except
there's suddenly no mystery any more. I've asked everyone
about it today, and they've all answered the same way, and with
total certainty. Here in Turin there's no controversy
whatsoever: Primo Levi committed suicide. And although the
family don't want it discussed (which family would?), and
although it doesn't feature in *Primo*, it haunts me. I no longer
need to know *if* he killed himself; now I just need to know *why*.
Was it because of Auschwitz? Is there a clue in his words at the
end of the chapter called 'The Last One'? 'To destroy a man is
difficult, almost as difficult as to create one: it has not been easy
or quick, but you Germans have succeeded . . . because we also
are broken, conquered . . . even if we have finally learned how
to find our food and to resist the fatigue and cold, even if we
return home.' *Even if we return home . . .*

Later I write another letter on the Grand Hotel stationery:

Dear Primo,
I visited your home today, but wasn't allowed in.
Roberto broke this surprising news as he parked in the
side street: Renzo had instructed him that we weren't to
enter the building, not even the lobby – especially not the
lobby.
As we tried to absorb this information – *we've come all
the way from London and can't even enter the building?* –
Roberto pointed up to a balcony. 'That's outside Primo's
study,' he said. Although I longed to see your writing
room, my main attention was on the height of the balcony
itself . . . only on the third floor, yet all the windows on
the apartment block are tall, the rooms are clearly tall . . .
three floors is high, high enough for you to do it and be
fairly sure of the result. Why didn't you do it here in the
street though, I wonder, from your balcony. Why do it
inside the house?
We walked round to the front door . . . so familiar from
photographs . . . though I never realised you lived on a busy
main road. Now came another surprise. The ground floor
is no longer an apartment – it's a solarium, a place open to
the public. Couldn't we just go in to the reception there,
and so see inside? When I said this to Roberto, he became
very uneasy, and kept glancing upwards. Was Lucia watching us through the third floor windows? Renzo too maybe,
from his apartment next to hers? As we stood there, a
woman wearing a white coat arrived at the door – one of
the solarium staff – unlocked it and went in. As the door
was slowly swinging shut, I instinctively reached out my
hand. I held it ajar. Roberto looked pale. 'Please be quick,'
he muttered, and then darted away, round the corner.
Richard and I hurried in. A stone entrance hall, a turn
to the right, and there it was. The lobby. By now I wasn't

expecting to see it, so I hadn't braced myself. Even if I had, it would've shocked me terribly. It was so narrow – I mean the space through which you fell, the area of floor you hit – so much of it taken up by the lift shaft and its cage. Did you hit the sides of this as you fell, did you hit the corners of the curving stairs? Did you take off your spectacles beforehand? I tried to imagine your flight . . . down through your home . . . the place where you were born, where you lived all your life . . . down through the core of it, the throat . . . did you scream as you went? Someone said this was your one howl of freedom. There are no howls in your writing. It's all so controlled. But now you are howling, you are free. This is my life, and I'll take it. But what violence you do to your house, to your family – you print a bloody ghost onto this piece of floor forever. I became very upset standing there, exactly on the spot where you landed – there was no choice, there was only space for one spot – it seemed as ugly as some of the spots we had stood on in Auschwitz. You had survived the Lager, incredibly, despite all its violence, and yet here, in the safety of your own home, every bone in your body was broken and your skull was smashed . . . though your face was intact, the reports say. I stood there, trembling and tearful, Richard took a couple of photos, and then we fled, feeling like thieves.

I understand now why your family didn't want us to see that place. It is terrible. But I won't be able to forget it.

With love,

Tony.

Sunday 5th September 2004

Curiouser and curiouser . . . Renzo's behaviour . . .

Last night Roberto treated us to dinner at a restaurant owned by friends, Sotto la Mole, next to Turin's bizarre trade-

mark tower, the Mole Antonelliana, which began life as a syna-
gogue and is now a cinema museum. Over dinner we took a
break from the subject of Primo. Greg was much taken with his
visit to the Turin Shroud ('You did the Jewish tour of the city,'
he said; 'I the Catholic one'), and Roberto's wife Flavia, a
warm, attractive woman, had intriguing observations about it.
But as we were leaving, I asked Roberto if he'd have one more
go at arranging a meeting with Renzo during the few hours
we've got left here in the morning – this morning, Sunday. The
original purpose of the visit was to meet the family, or at least
Renzo, who'd read the script personally, and sent his blessing
to the project. You can often glimpse a parent in their child –
this was certainly true when I met Stanley Spencer's daughters
– so I was very keen to see and talk with Renzo. By now I felt
that Roberto had grown to like and trust us. Couldn't he convey this to Renzo, and preside over a meeting? He said he'd try.

This morning I woke wondering what I'll say to Renzo if we
meet. I must keep it uncontroversial. I'm curious to ask if he's
named after Lorenzo, the Italian civilian worker in Auschwitz
who saved Primo's life by smuggling an extra ration of soup to
him every day.

When Primo returned home after his incarceration, he
sought out Lorenzo, and did much to help him: he was from an
impoverished rural family. But despite Lorenzo's heroism in
Auschwitz, the place had traumatised him. And the charac-
teristics which Primo first noted in him – 'silent, morose, often
smelling of wine' – eventually destroyed him: he died of drink,
aged 47.

The phone rings. It's Roberto. He's just spoken to Renzo,
who wanted to know everything about yesterday's tour, and
about us: 'I got the impression he really wanted to meet you . . .
he was really tempted . . . but when I suggested it, he said he
had other arrangements this morning. But then he asked me to
give you his number. I think if you ring him now, you might
persuade him . . . '

After Roberto's call, I sit staring at Renzo's number, and at the phone. Something stops me picking it up. It's all getting too complicated. I thought the family's attitude to us this weekend was being dictated by Lucia (forbidding us to enter the building was something an old woman might decide, rather than a forty-something university lecturer), but now I'm not so sure. The way Renzo keeps blowing hot-cold, hot-cold. Something comes back to me. On the morning of Primo's suicide, the concierge was cleaning the entrance hall when she heard a noise in the lobby . . . and as soon as she saw the body, it was Renzo whom she first summoned. How would you ever get over that? Our visit seems to have stirred up disturbing things for him and the family. We should leave them alone now, leave them in peace. We should respect the fact that, although the name Primo Levi might seem like public property to us, to them it simply conjures up a husband and father. And anyway, even without meeting them this visit has been invaluable.

So I don't pick up the phone. We spend the morning strolling along the River Po, then lunch at the hotel, before heading out to the airport. At a clothes shop in the departure lounge, Richard and I buy a tie which might be suitable for my costume – it would be good to wear something from Turin. Yesterday evening, we bought another in a shop near the hotel. It was better than this one, but when we examined at it later we saw that it was made in New York.

Monday 6th September 2004

Two weeks to go.

Woke with this realisation, and didn't like it. The Turin trip has been standing as a kind of safety barrier between me and the reality of doing the show, and now that it's over there's a new countdown.

Good day. I've started wearing rehearsal clothes – shirt, tie, sleeveless cardie – as well as the actual shoes and glasses that

I'll wear in performance. The tie particularly helps to constrict me, and helps me become the little professor, the chemist. Also, after what I've learned in Turin over the weekend (and I don't think I've ever known more about a character, not even S. Spencer), I can work with positives rather than negatives. It's no longer a case of *don't* colour, *don't* press too hard, *don't* act; now it's *do* be reserved, *do* be contained, *do* conceal feelings – *this is what he was like*. At the end of the day, we ran the first four sections. It felt very weird again, but Richard was pleased. Then we watched a new documentary, which the Holocaust Education Trust found for us . . .

Dear Primo,
  I finally met you today.
  For weeks we've been chasing you. Chasing documentaries where you might appear. Bizarrely, you never do. Or just in silence, or just too briefly. Anyway, this afternoon I finally saw you properly and heard you talking – in fluent English – for about an hour, and you looked like the famous Primo that I know (specs, grey beard), the one I'm trying to play. This was a BBC Bookmark programme you made while you were here in London in 1985, promoting the British publication of *The Periodic Table*.
  You are surprising. You have a twinkle. You are gentle, sweet, humorous. I dare not use those words to Richard – he'll fear that I'll caricature them (he fears my acting, full-stop) – but you are also 'open', so at least he's right about that.
  I stared and stared at you – searching for the depressive, the man who would hurl himself down a stairwell two years after this film – but couldn't see him.
  I liked you, I liked you a lot. I'm relieved about that.
  With love,
  Tony.

Tuesday 7th September 2004

I said to Richard this morning: 'After seeing Primo himself yesterday, a new thought occurs. I was surprised how good his English was . . . '

'Indeed,' said Richard.

' . . . And I began to wonder: should we be playing him in an Italian accent?'

'Hmm . . . I wondered about that too.'

We look at one another. This would be a major new factor. I'm very particular about accents. I don't just carry round a bunch of used ones in my pocket. If I'm doing an accent, I like to study it carefully with one of the dialect experts like Joan Washington or Andrew Jack. With only two weeks to go, can I take on this extra work load?

Richard spoke slowly, thinking aloud: 'The trouble with an accent . . . even if it's done well, and, knowing you I'm sure it would be, but . . . it's "acting" . . . it's "theatrical" somehow . . . it would be a tiny barrier between you and the audience . . . between you and the character, actually. I want people to hear *you* talking – I want them to think these things happened to *you*.'

'Yes,' I said, feeling relieved; 'I think we'll leave it as it is, then.'

'I think we will.'

Today we started feeding in some music – just recorded pieces for now (in performance it'll be live, apart from the Auschwitz band). Richard and Jonathan the composer have convinced me that the cello is right, and Jonathan has found a selection of Piedmontese folk tunes which are beautiful and haunting rather than solemn and portentous.

Our designer Hildegard sat in for an afternoon run of 5, 6, 7, 8. I noticed an immediate onset of small nervous signs in myself – from time to time a shiver in my voice, in my hand on one gesture, and even in my legs. With a new person watching, I began to worry that Richard's insistence on 'no colouring' has led to a soporific evenness, but Hildegard said she found it powerful.

Afterwards, a private discussion with Richard about a delicate matter. As a note-taker during run-throughs, he has one strength and one weakness. The strength is that he tells you beforehand that he won't write the note on the moment – it can be very distracting when you see directors suddenly scribbling notes (*what have I just done wrong?*), and only an actor-director would've thought up a way of cushioning the process. His weakness is that he doesn't stay in his chair during the action: he stands or walks about. I said I didn't mind the walking about – which is done quite sensitively – all I was requesting is that he carry his notebook with him. There were times today when he had to scurry back to the table to jot notes, and I did find this unnecessarily disturbing. So now I was giving him a note (*please just carry the book with you*), and directors don't like getting notes – I know it, I live with one – and indeed Richard took it rather grumpily. For a man who's favourite word is 'open', he's sometimes quite the opposite.

Wednesday 8th September 2004

Woke at 6am to do lines, feeling exhausted and edgy. Today we're running sections 1–8. And on Friday we're doing our first complete run. I requested this; Richard wasn't going to try a run yet. But I have to experience the marathon this week – before next week, which is our last.

Today's mini-run was OK. Richard was very pleased. (He carried his notebook with him as he walked about – hooray – my first victory!) Paul Pyant, who watched, talked of 'the power of storytelling.' He also mentioned my 'matter-of-fact' tone – intending this as praise, yet worrying me. Telling Primo's story never feels matter-of-fact.

When I do it, my overwhelming sense is still of floating in space, and of the distinctive stillness which the material engenders in anyone who's listening. It's like what Primo describes on the railway platform when they arrive at Auschwitz:

'Everything was as silent as an aquarium, or as in certain dream sequences . . . '

News of Hitler back at home. The *Churchill* film is no longer opening on Yom Kippur, thank God, but in December. I think Peter Richardson (director and writer) and Jonathan Cavendish (producer) have fallen out. During the editing of the film, Peter departed and Jonathan did a cut. But then Peter showed his own cut to the American stars (Chris and Neve), and they liked it. So then Jonathan departed, and Peter was reinstated. The film world is not one I understand. Anyway, I'm relieved. There was something crazy about me opening as Primo and Hitler on the same day, Yom Kippur or not.

Thursday 9th September 2004

In the morning, a Marietta session. A good one. We tackled The Fear. There's no-one else, not even Greg, with whom I can discuss this completely frankly, the full extent of it, how close it's brought me to fleeing the stage mid-performance – doing an Ian Holm – or no, worse, giving up acting completely. So, what about *Primo*? The first public performance is fifteen days away. I have fifteen days to get rid of the thing. And there's no middle ground with this one. A one-man show is already as frightening as acting gets. If you add The Fear it's impossible. So I either perform it without The Fear or I don't perform it at all. Never mind an Ian Holm, it's a Stephen Fry I'll be doing, and boarding the next ferry for Belgium.

Marietta and I had something of a breakthrough, I think. We were discussing Primo's death. I said that after everything I'd read, and everyone I'd spoken to – especially in Turin – I now believed two things. Yes it was suicide, no it wasn't Auschwitz claiming him forty years later. Or not directly, anyway. His last and fatal depression seemed to have been caused by a combination of factors: a recent prostate operation, the presence of

his mother in the apartment – very ill, but still very powerful –
and, perhaps most significantly, the rise of Neo-Fascism in
Europe. Maybe it wasn't Auschwitz which killed him, but the
threat of its return. This coincided with a recurring nightmare,
which he reports at the end of *The Truce*: the normal, safe,
civilised world melts away from around him, and he's back in
the Lager, he's back forever. I said to Marietta: 'He probably
had a suicidal nature, and it might even be in his genes – his
grandfather killed himself, jumping out of a window – but
whether so or not, he's definitely a depressive. Before Auschwitz, after Auschwitz, but not *in* Auschwitz. He could just run
against the nearest electric fence and finish things there and
then, but somehow he doesn't.'

'That's right, because there's no room for his depression in
Auschwitz,' said Marietta; 'Auschwitz is as bad as it gets, it's a
living nightmare. Every scrap of his energy has to go into fighting it. There's no room for his own demons. No need for them.'

What a thought. That we *need* our demons. In some situations, and not in others. No room for them. So is there a clue
here? There was no room for Primo's demons in Auschwitz.
There is no room for mine in *Primo*. Is it as simple as that? Is
it just a question of mental will? Because Primo does make a
choice in Auschwitz, however subconsciously: he chooses *not* to
give in to depression. Can I just choose *not* to have stage fright?

I know there's no comparison between the fear of going
onstage and fighting for your life in Auschwitz, but I don't
care, I'm going to use this to help me.

In the afternoon, we prepared for tomorrow's run, our first.
I felt strangely excited about it. Which isn't like me at all.

Friday 10th September 2004

Dear Primo,

Before today's run, I created a little talisman of you
next to my briefcase: one of your school reports which

they gave us in Turin, and the three stones we collected in
Auschwitz, one from each camp. I'm not sure you'd approve of me representing you like this, but I just needed
something to touch before launching myself into the void.

That sounds like a fall down a stairwell again . . .
anyway, I didn't fall . . . it was more like flying.

It was OK. The run was OK. Still weird and dream-
like, but OK. Good to have a little audience: Hildegard,
Jonathan Goldstein, the sound guy Rich Walsh. I looked
them in the eye as I spoke, which made a nice change from
talking to walls.

I dried three times, and asked for and took prompts
calmly, while getting an inner fright on each occasion. What
if I dry in performance, where there'll be no prompt? In
the Cottesloe, the man with the script, the man running
the show – ASM Thomas – sits in a booth at the back of
the auditorium, so he can't prompt. But what if I need
one? It doesn't bear thinking about. There was no onset of
The Fear today, but I knew there wouldn't be. That only
comes in performance. Or used to come. We'll see. That's
a test ahead of me.

Richard has curtailed all the occurrences of emotion in
the piece. On the one hand I've resented this, on the other
hand I know he's right. When I wrote the script, and in
the early days of learning lines, I cried constantly. But
that was me crying for you. You never cry for you.

But Alberto . . . did you cry for Alberto? When I got to
his death today, I had a huge struggle. My voice cracked
as I said the line, and then I couldn't carry on for several
moments – just sat there, head down, fighting tears. In a
way, it was exactly right: when we watched those documentaries, the survivors often wanted to cry, but stopped
themselves, or cried silently, without tears or noise, cried
inwardly.

At the end, the little audience applauded, and were very complimentary. Actually they didn't have to say anything – I had felt the impact of the piece on them. They sat so still.

Afterwards, we had a costume fitting up in Wardrobe. This was much better than last time, and we were all in total agreement . . . ! Captured just the right un-English, academic look: the Italian shoes from Harrods, the tie from Turin (though made in New York), a pair of yellowish fawn trousers, grey sleeveless cardie, blue shirt, and the big glasses exactly like yours. Even though I haven't cut my hair and beard to your style yet, quite a resemblance is already emerging. It could end up as good as Stanley Spencer.

Stanley is often in my mind these days, because that was the last time I performed in this building, and it was a big success. I'm hoping some of that will pass like magic dust through the atmosphere and brush off onto *Primo*. I remember Richard Eyre asking me why I seemed to be inhabiting Stanley more than anything he'd seen me do, and I replied, 'I don't know, I just love him.' Richard said, 'Yes of course – it's always about love.' And that's been the big turning point on this show as well: the moment Marietta said, 'Why don't you do this one out of love.'

Talking of *Stanley* I bumped into Debbie Findlay (who played Stanley's first wife Hilda) at the stage door as I was leaving; she's here rehearsing *The Mandate*. I gave her a lift to Islington – she lives nearby – and she popped into our house first. We sat in the kitchen, where we used to learn *Stanley* lines together, helping to create Stan and Hilda's symbiotic relationship, and had a long chat. Just what I needed after today's run.

When Greg got home from Stratford, I was working away happily down in my study, doing cuts; the run was 1 hour 37 minutes, which is about 15 minutes too long.

He said, 'So how was it?' I said, 'Yes, OK I think.' He grinned at me, sensing that it was more than that.

With love,

Tony.

Saturday 11th September 2004

Dear Primo,

Writing to you on the anniversary of 9/11 seems apt somehow. I wrote to another friend today – Simon Callow – using one of the postcards we bought in Auschwitz, and said, 'What are friends for if you can't send them a postcard from Auschwitz on 9/11?'

I saw you in Auschwitz the other day, by the way. That Italian documentary they made when you went back in '81 – Roberto gave us a copy last weekend in Turin. There's a shot of you getting off the coach, and approaching the Arbeit Macht Frei gate. If it shocks me, that gate, I don't know what it does to you. The camera comes in for a close-up. Nothing shows in your face, nothing. Yet one feels it inside you. Exactly like Richard says I should play you. He's right about that. He's right about (almost) everything, damn him.

With love,

Tony.

Sunday 12th September 2004

Spoke to Mom this evening. I mentioned that we lunched with the Blakes today – those good people who've been like guardian parents ever since I arrived in this country – and I said how well they were looking. Mom seemed to know who they were, and said she'd ring them – did I have their number? As I read it out, and as she transcribed it laboriously, and as I explained she'd have to drop the 0 from the 0208 prefix, I became aware that we both knew she wouldn't actually make the call. I felt a sense of shame (the Primo Levi word) that we were even going through the motions. Illness is a form of humiliation, of imprisonment.

Monday 13th September 2004

One week to go.

The other evening, when Debbie was here, she glanced out of the window at the garden, hesitated, then said quietly, 'Oh it's autumn.'

That's undoubtedly true this morning – dark, wet, windy – adding to my routine Monday morning blues.

We spent the day rehearsing the new cuts, so it wasn't too pressurised. At lunchtime, we heard that Harriet Walter was front-of-house, making preparations for the 'do' here tomorrow evening: a celebration for her partner, the actor Peter Blythe, who died in June, and would've been 70 tomorrow. We went to find her. This was the first time I'd seen her since Peter's death. She was perfectly composed, in good spirits actually, yet there was something altered deep within her.

Afterwards, as we walked along the Thames, I said to Richard, 'That was like another acting lesson for playing Primo – someone back in the normal world after they've been through a real-life nightmare. She never showed a flicker of grief, yet I felt very moved.'

Everything, *everything* feeds the work at the moment.

Later . . .

Dear Primo,

A bad thing happened tonight.

I've been losing weight to play you. Even though I won't be appearing in prisoner mode, as one of the living skeletons you describe, I still feel your whole shape, indeed your very character, is trimmer than mine. On Friday morning, the day of the run-through, I was delighted when the bathrom scales showed I'd reached my target weight: 12 stone. Quite an achievement in comparison to Tsafendas (13 st 4lbs) and even Iago (12st 10lbs), and in fact it's the lightest I've been in years.

But during the costume fitting later that afternoon, Richard started making disparaging remarks about my weight. It was just joshing between friends, but it got to me. I wondered whether, to get the perfect look, I might have to lose even more?

Tonight I got home to find that Greg had cooked my favourite dish for supper: tomato bredie, a South African lamb stew, from a recipe taught to him by Katie (Roberts, our family cook). It was a particularly delicious one – he'd let it simmer for hours – and was washed down with an equally fine Gévrey-Chambertin. But I felt guilty about consuming all these calories. As I was going to bed, my guilt suddenly got the better of me, so I snuck down to the basement loo, and made myself throw up. I immediately felt terrible about this. First of all, because Greg had worked hard to give me a special treat during this testing time, but, more importantly, because of you. You are starving, dying of hunger, literally – and I, playing you, had just made myself regurgitate beautiful food and wine . . . !

No. This is unacceptable, this is disgusting. It weighs heavy on me. (Heavier than any calories.)

I must be careful. The pressures of this show are unique. And Richard is too much in control. My every gesture, my every thought, my weight for God's sake. I've been grateful for his vision in staging his piece; it's remarkable – and I had no vision at all. But now we must get to the point where this thing becomes mine. Not his – mine. In other words – yours. Shit, this gets complicated.

In the meantime, I apologise for tonight.
With love,
Tony.

Tuesday 14th September 2004

We did a second run. Very good. I didn't dry once, and the cuts resulted in a running time which was 10 minutes shorter: 1 hour 27 minutes.

Afterwards, a constructive discussion (perhaps triggered by last night's craziness, which of course I never mentioned). Richard keeps asking for more and more understatement, and is couching it in a new way: 'Be more Primo.' Today I said maybe we had different ideas about Primo, and whenever Richard says, 'Be more Primo', I actually hear, 'Be more Richard.' I said, 'When I first read the book, I found it shocking, upsetting, illuminating, and uplifting – probably in that order – and unless the show has a similar effect on the audience, we'll have failed. If they're just going to sit there thinking, "So that's what life was like in Auschwitz, how interesting", we'll have failed.' Richard conceded that we'd have to let the preview audiences teach us, and may indeed have to do more in the end, but meanwhile he wanted us to be brave, and continue along these lines . . .

After rehearsals, an event which put everything in perspective: Harriet's celebration of Peter's life. He did a lot of work at the National, so it was fitting to hold it here, in the Terrace Café. An impressive turn-out, including Peter Hall, Tom Stoppard, David Edgar, Simon Callow, David Suchet, Tim West, Pru Scales, and even a critic, John Peter. Harriet asked Greg to be the MC, so he invited us to watch a compilation of Peter's film clips, and also joined with Harriet to read some of the tributes which were sent in for the funeral. Beforehand, Harriet wasn't sure she'd be able to get through it, and an 'understudy' was standing alongside (her friend, Kate Littlewood), but Harriet did, and it was only at the very end, as she stepped off the little dais, that I saw her close her eyes and cover her mouth. God knows what this must feel like for her (unimaginable to me, in terms of Greg), but for the rest of us there was a pervading atmosphere of poignancy, along with much laughter and some tears.

Among the throng, I found several one-man-show veterans: Noma Dumezwani (who did *The Bogus Woman* at the Bush), David Suchet (who did *The Kreutzer Sonata* and *Brief Lives*), and especially Simon Callow (who's performed about six and directed about two). David and Simon both said exactly the same thing: 'After doing this, you'll never want to be in an ordinary play again.' I felt puzzled by this. Although I haven't been in front of an audience yet, I know this won't be true for me. I guess all other one-man shows have more interaction, more laughter than *Primo*, which just creates this weird sense of floating in electrified space. Simon gave me several good tips, especially this one: 'You must understand that rehearsing a one-man show is much, much harder than playing it. In performance, you'll finally get the other character, someone to tell the story to, an audience.'

Wednesday 15th September 2004

Whole day spent with Jonathan Goldstein and a cellist, Nick, who won't be our actual one – he isn't available till next week. We did all the musical links, and also some experiments: with a little help from the sound department, the cello can do very good impressions of a dripping tap, the rhythm of train wheels, and a thump for distant artillery. Richard wants to keep actual sound effects to an absolute minimum: just the reveille bell, the end-of-work siren, and the winter wind, since these are all arguably musical sounds, and might feasibly be used in modern compositions. The pressure was off me again, and I thoroughly enjoyed the collaborative creative process: us all working together to find the right soundscape.

Thursday 16th September 2004

Another run. With a bigger audience. As well as the creative team, there was our producer Pádraig Cusack, the voice coach Patsy Rodenburg, Lyn Haill (from the programme-design dept.), and Tim Levey, assistant to Nick II. Nick himself is on holiday (inbetween opening *Stuff Happens* and re-rehearsing *His Dark Materials*) and won't see us till one of the previews. I take it as a sign of trust that he feels able to go away while we open. But I'm also aware that several of the people here today – Pádraig and Tim certainly – will be e-mailing him later with their reactions. This is the moment when the show's reputation, good or bad, spreads through the building.

The run went well, and was even shorter – just 1 hour 22 minutes. I dried only once, and so briefly no-one even knew. As Simon said the other night, it was a relief to have people to tell the story to. And it had the required effect. Patsy said how 'fine' it was, and that Primo's inner life was 'amazing'. She said it makes it tougher for an audience: they feel they're in the presence of someone who's really been through it. Lyn said something similar: the restraint makes it more moving, more shocking. Pádraig was very complimentary too: he said he thought Primo himself would approve. And when I was leaving through the stage door, there was a most unexpected and touching card from Tim Levey: he said *If This Is A Man* is a very important book for him, and he felt Richard and I have 'more than honoured it'.

I think the e-mails to Nick tonight are going to be OK.

The only bad news came from Hildegard, and it had nothing to do with the design: apparently, one part of my German pronunciation is wrong, and it's crucial – my tatooed number, 174517. I'm not good with languages (the only other one I learned at school was Afrikaans), so I tried to master the number ages ago, in the Workshop, but it seems I got it wrong. When I reached home this evening, I stuck sheets of paper on the bathroom mirror, in my study, even the front door, with the new correct pronunciation, written in my own phonetics: *Hun-dirt feer und seeb-tzig finf hundirt seeb-tzane.*

Friday 17th September 2004

Dear Primo,

Officially the last day of rehearsals and officially our last run. (Though we'll do two more next week – we don't actually start the tech till Wednesday evening.) Among today's little invited audience were two very significant people, a couple of actors from the Workshop: Christoph and Elliot. Good to have them there – people who were in on the start of this journey. I was particularly moved to see Elliot's face during the run. It held an expression I remembered from those awful 'punishment exercises' at the Studio when he was my fellow prisoner. Normally Elliot has a permanent smile, but this vanished when he was intimidated by the German guards, and suddenly he looked pale and stunned. The same thing happened today during the run. Like you, like me, Elliot is not a believer, and yet what you experienced was somehow so profoundly Jewish that one can't read it or hear it told without feeling a tremendous personal shock. Afterwards, Elliot said he found it mesmerising.

I drove home over Blackfrairs Bridge – a light lovely evening, with London sprawling out lazily on either side – and felt an intense sensation of happiness. Not just that all the work seems to be paying off, but also that I stand a chance of conquering The Fear on this. I've been strangely calm before each of the runs, strangely peaceful, and if I was a spiritualist (like Mom) I would've said it was your presence. The feeling is almost like being in love. Would you be embarrassed by this metaphor, I wonder. Would you mind the fact that I, a gay actor, am playing you? In rehearsals we discussed whether you might be gay. I don't think so, despite the importance of a whole line of significant male friends in your life: Alberto of course (Dalla Volta), and also the first Alberto (Salmoni), and Leonardo (De Benedetti), Charles (Conreau), and even those two reprobates in *The Truce*, The Greek and Cesare. I think you had a shy relationship with women – a cruel boy at school tells you that circumcision equals castration – and a troubled and puritanical attitude to sex. Yet you get on famously when Philip Roth comes to visit (we're using some of your conversation in our programme), and I love the idea of the grave Holocaust witness meeting the dirty American novelist. There was much laughter apparently. You dined with him at the Cambio, where we dined on our first night in Turin: you and Lucia, him and his then wife, Claire Bloom. (A Hollywood star, the actress from *Limelight* – you Levis were so excited!) I'd love to have been a fly on the wall . . .

Anyway, an exquisite lightness of being this evening, despite what awaits this time next week. The first public performance. On Yom Kippur.

With love,

Tony.

Part Five

Doing Primo

Saturday 18th September 2004

Today, it was a relief not to work on *Primo*. Decided to even leave the lines alone, and might do the same tomorrow. Instead a day of treats. In the morning I popped to the Wine Warehouse and spent a sinful amount of money stocking up on favourite Burgundies, white and red. In the afternoon we went to *A Funny Thing Happened on the Way to the Forum* at the Olivier. Actually this wasn't as much of a treat as we were hoping. Despite terrific work from the company, the musical itself is pretty feeble, and there's only one hit number. Apparently the cast use our rehearsal room for their warm-up, and find it very odd singing 'Comedy Tonight' surrounded by images of Auschwitz.

Sunday 19th September 2004

A relaxed day – a walk on Hampstead Heath, a lunch at the Almeida Restaurant – but all the time, a small tense feeling, a beating pulse, a ticking clock . . . the countdown has started . . .

This time next week, I'll have done it. Twice. Jesus.

When I spoke to Mom she sounded chirpy. During the week, my brother Randall went to view a Bantry Bay apartment on my behalf – for when I do *Primo* in Cape Town – and Mom seemed to have an awareness of this. Said she was 'counting the days'. I asked her to keep her fingers crossed for me next week, and felt sad that she would forget to.

Monday 20th September 2004

It is the week. It is *this* week.

I value what I can. I say to myself, 'Monday's better than Tuesday because there's no audience at the run today, no pressure.' Tomorrow I'll say, 'Tuesday's better than Wednesday because I've got a last night of freedom.' And so on. Everything to put safety barriers between me and Friday. But hopefully when Friday comes I'll welcome it.

Spent the morning working with our cellist, our real one, Robin Thompson-Clarke. A decent, warm chap, with bright light in dark eyes, and like all musicians blessed with a slightly different wavelength from the rest of us . . . connected to the music of the spheres. It's a relief to have someone else onstage with me (he'll be to one side, behind a screen), and with a script. If the worst happened, might he prompt . . . ?

There is an audience at today's run – an audience of one. The actor John Light, who's in *Night Season*. He asked if he could come and see it, because he played Stefan in Sean Holmes' excellent revival of *Singer* at the Tricycle earlier this year, and just like in our original production, the cast were encouraged to read *If This Is A Man*. Before the run, John said he was anticipating it with great curiosity – he couldn't imagine how the book might work on stage. After the run, he tried to thank and compliment us, but he couldn't speak, his eyes were full. When he left the room, I said to Richard, 'That's our best review so far.'

Dear Primo,

This afternoon ended with me in the Wig Room, getting my beard cut to your style – a goatee with tapering sides – and my hair to your shape: brushed back. Spent two happy hours, pouring over photos of you, the wig lady, Gill Blair, proceeding carefully stage by stage, Hildegard and Hattie watching, advising, chatting. I told them this was a lucky room for me – it's where we first achieved the *Stanley* transformation. And indeed the same thing happened today. After my beard, moustache and hair were trimmed, I greyed them up, popped on the glasses, and there you were. It's as near as dammit.

With love,

Tony.

Tuesday 21st September 2004

Marietta session. These have become exceptional. We've been working together for eight years now, but we're suddenly in new territory, covering new ground. It's because of The Fear. *Primo* is make-or-break time.

Ever since I saw the lobby at 75 Corso Re Umberto, I've felt compelled to draw Primo's flight down the stairwell: seen from above, his feet in the foreground, the viewer dropping with him, down through the centre of his home, the place he's known all his life – birth channel, death channel – down, down, banging the lift cage, the sharp edges of the stairs, a swirling vortex, down, down, down. But something troubles me about doing this. I'm scared of portraying all that negativity, revelling in it to some extent. The fall ends in a crash, in destruction. I can't let myself go that way, not this week – not even in a drawing.

When this morning's session started, I discussed it with Marietta. She half encouraged me to do the suicide drawing, on the basis that it's better to offload such things here, in the safety of her room. But I said I had a strong feeling that I mustn't do it. I must find an opposite image, a positive image, an image of hope. She said: 'Well, go with your feeling. You're making a choice – that's good – you're maybe finding there's more choice in things than you think.'

I ended up drawing an image of Primo and myself, hands linked, moving forward with purpose and strength, heading towards a doorway or opening, which I labelled 'Friday' – the first preview. Two figures, stronger for being two, a twinship . . . like Primo and Alberto, or me and Greg . . . Friday coming up, and me *not alone*.

Unfortunately I had trouble sketching the hands: the linked hands. Which of whose fingers go where? And is it my right hand, his left hand, or vice versa? I made a real mess of it, and that was a pity since it was the most important part of the image for me. But instead of raging – which I'd normally do – I began to laugh. Marietta was intrigued, and asked why. I said I thought Primo would've laughed. As the chemist, the scientist, the meticulous man, he would've known how important those hands were, but the other side of him, the side with the twinkle (in the Bookmark documentary), the side that had fun with Philip Roth, the side which understood about human fallibility – that side would've laughed.

I think I surprised Marietta today. Which you can't often do with someone who knows you inside out (literally). Actually, I think I surprised myself.

Drove to work feeling empowered. Mom used to have a book called something like *The Power of Positive Thinking*, which she always urged me to read. I resisted, instinctively mistrusting that American brand of sermonising psycho-babble. But maybe there's something in the concept – the power of positive thinking – even if it isn't easy for a committed pessimist like myself.

This afternoon's run, our sixth and the last in the rehearsal room, was the best yet. I felt calm and in control. The timing was 1 hour 24 minutes. Among today's audience was Jack Bradley, the Literary Manager, and the hero of the rights-acquiring battle. He was full of praise, and confirmed what others have: the restraint makes it more shocking, more moving. I gave full credit to Richard. And not just for how he's directed my performance – I think he's creating a truly impressive production, way beyond anything I imagined, and we haven't even got the set yet, the lights, and other effects.

Before leaving the building, I peeked into the Cottesloe. The set was being assembled onstage, the auditorium was dotted with work tables and console desks, and the whole place was swarming with people: climbing ladders, carrying things, laying cables.

Jesus, I thought, all this for a one-man show.

Dear Primo,

Came home very happy, to enjoy my last night of freedom. Unfortunately the Channel 4 News was grisly. Three men were kidnapped in Iraq a few days ago, two Americans and a Brit. One of the Americans was murdered yesterday – by beheading, which was videoed and shown on an Arab website – and the family of the Brit, a Liverpudlian called Kenneth Bigley, has spent today begging the British government to help them. Halfway through the bulletin, news came that the second American had been beheaded as well. I sat in front of the telly stunned – Greg was downstairs preparing supper. My mind filled with images of selections . . . will you die, yes or no? When Greg brought the tray up, he found me in tears. He said, 'Is this the show?' I said no, then said yes.

With love,
Tony.

Wednesday 22nd September 2004

The tech doesn't start till this evening, so I've got the day off.

Begin by re-doing the drawing of Primo and me with hands

linked, moving together towards Friday. Using our digital
camera, I manage to photograph my hand holding Greg's, and
this becomes the reference for that confusing tangle of fingers.
Quite pleased by the result. Might get photocopies made, and
use them as my first night card.

Soon realise I'm too jumpy to stay at home. I drive to the
theatre, and go through all the lines, pacing round the empty
rehearsal room, where the walls have been stripped of all our
photos and maps. The only remnant is one sheet of paper fallen
to the floor, with my German phonetics: *Hundirt feer und seeb-
tzig finf hundirt seeb-tzane.* Then I wander along the Thames,
thinking of all those lunchtime walks with Richard, and remembering how warm and sunny the weather was at the beginning of rehearsals. August and September have flown by.

I lunch at a restaurant on Gabriel's Wharf, in an upstairs
room full of light and air, overlooking the river. I have a new
constant companion these days, another veteran of the solo
show, though an unexpected one – David Hare. I'm reading
Acting Up, his book about doing *Via Dolorosa*, the piece he
wrote and performed about his trip to Israel. Richard had
mentioned it was a good read, and it is, even if you missed the
show as I did. David writes eloquently of course, and it's full
of wit and insight and plain good advice; I've learned a valuable
tip from his voice doctor – a little bite of your tongue produces
instant saliva. It's also blazingly honest, and all the funnier for
it. He's trying to learn a new skill – acting – yet goes at it with
the humility of a charging rhino. He fights and fumes with
everyone in sight, from his director to his audience. It makes
me seem like a model of composure. On the other hand, maybe
his way is better? He lets off steam – the peculiar pressure of a
one-man show – while I hold it in, which leads to bad dreams,
or me rehearsing rows with Richard which I never have. Well,
if we're swopping roles, with David straying into acting and me
into playwriting, maybe I'll save my explosions for playwriting.
Towards the beginning, David quotes Camus who says you

should only go to a doctor who has your disease. In the same way, currently there's nothing I want to do more with my spare time than read David's book.

At 6pm I do the make-up, a procedure I enjoy in every show, perhaps enjoy most; it's like painting a portrait. At 6.45 Gill comes down from the Wig Room to do the bits I can't: greying the back of my hair, and stencilling on my Auschwitz number. It's odd watching someone do this with gentleness and care. Then I get into costume, and stroll down to the Cottesloe, feeling calm, yet braced for action; I'm about to embark on the last and most testing part of this journey.

Just before the tech starts, I ask stage manager Ernie to show me where Michael Bryant's brick is. After he died, a brick was dislodged in each of the National's three auditoria, and a portion of his ashes sealed inside. I've learned this from his widow, Judy Coke, who's written me a kind note, wishing me well, and promising that Mike will watch over me. Ernie takes me over to the back of the stage – stage left. The real brick wall is covered by a wall of our set, yet Ernie is able to point exactly to the spot where Mike is resting. I love this idea. I've always said that the walls of theatres are full of ghosts, good ghosts, actors' ghosts, and here we really do have one.

At 7 o'clock we're off. Again there's the shock of quite a large crowd of workers out in the auditorium, and only me onstage. The first hour or so is very disorientating: the darkness, the light changes, even the edge of the stage, which has a four-foot drop, and induces a slight balance wobble, like during *Othello* in Japan. All actors experience a recurring nightmare, the actor's nightmare, in which they're in a play, yet they've never rehearsed it, never spoken the lines before – and now I feel it's happening for real. Then I reassure myself: this sensation isn't only familiar from bad dreams – the start of *every* tech feels like this. It's the jolt of moving from the big, bright, comfy, old rehearsal room to a hushed and dark auditorium where the atmosphere is very concentrated and precise, with everyone focused on their dials and switches: should that lighting effect be up a point, should that sound cue come in one word earlier? The only difference tonight is that I don't have other actors round me. We'd be saying to one another, 'God, this feels weird, doesn't it?' And this is where you have to admire David Hare's bravery. (He hates it when people call him brave, but never mind – he is.) He didn't have the benefit of our years and years of experience. At this point, for example, he would've had no way of reassuring himself that he hadn't landed on Mars.

But after the initial trauma of techs, I usually love them: no acting required, a chance to relax, fool around a bit. Tonight is simply exhausting though. Four hours of me repeating bits again and again, or waiting while they tinker with this or that. Also, while I perform sections, they whisper urgently among themselves out there in the blackness, which makes it hard to concentrate. I tell myself all these obstacles are good – like Richard walking around during run-throughs – they all toughen me, they all prepare me for the task ahead.

But there are also moments when everyone out there goes silent. This was Primo's power working, not mine. (I must write and tell him.) Even with all the distractions of the tech, there are nevertheless occasions when his story shocks them rigid, makes them go still.

Thursday 23rd September 2004

Was given the morning off again – so they can catch up with lighting – and was looking forward to a lie-in. But of course 6am found me wide awake, lying on my back, staring at the ceiling like an electrocuted rabbit. Told myself that at least today – tech and dress rehearsal – isn't as bad as tomorrow: another dress rehearsal and first preview. Tomorrow I'll (probably) tell myself it isn't as bad as next Thursday: press night. Next

Thursday I'll (hopefully) tell myself it's a pleasure and a privilege doing this show, and nothing's bad at all.

Yesterday I forgot to mention that Hildegard's set is remarkable. Surprisingly big, surprisingly epic. Three-quarters across the back wall, it suddenly has a second, slightly deeper plane, creating an odd little corner. This will be the location for one of the most important moments in the piece, when Primo is jammed in by the naked crowd as they all wait for the selection. The sealed door in this area is immensely disturbing; it looks like you could chip and tear at it for a hundred years and never get through. The other, wider opening on the set leads to freedom, although you can't see this; you just see another wall further back, and the floor here is littered with low heaps of unspecific but sinister waste – human ashes or hair? The whole environment is certainly possessed of that quality Richard wanted – a cruel beauty. When the tech resumed today, I told Hildegard that she should enter it for the Turner Prize, as one of those modern art installations. I was serious. Since all the boundaries are blurred now, with video and pottery qualifying for the Turner, why not a stage set?

Everyone says the costume works well against it, the modern-day costume – it's us (you and me) not them (walking skeletons in striped uniforms), so you have to go there yourself, go to Auschwitz, and you have to ask: how would *I* survive in this place?

Paul's lighting is also superb – every now and then Richard invites me down into the stalls to have a look – it's harsh, sometimes in squares with sharp edges (Dr Pannwitz's office, the lab) but again oddly beautiful. My only worry is that there's too much of it, it's too busy – cues are changing all the time.

This evening when Richard comes to my dressing room before the dress rehearsal, I raise this issue: 'Uhm . . . only one slight worry . . . I think Paul's lighting is terrific, but why has he not been given the Richard Wilson Lecture on Minimalism?'

He shrugs. 'Well, the audience might need a little help.'

I'm so stunned I don't reply. After he's gone, I start laughing aloud – imagining what the reply might've been in David Hare charging-rhino mode:

'The audience might need a little help? Oh fine. So I can now do my whinging old Yiddisher turn as Schmulek and my Little Hitler as Alex. And Hildegard can throw swathes of barbed wire over the set, along with the odd guard tower. And Jonathan can start underscoring the action with violins that'll break your heart. Oh fine, if the audience need a little help, let's give it to 'em!'

The truth of the matter is that I'm not sure if I'm right about the lighting. It's impossible to tell from where I'm standing. I'll have to wait till outsiders see the show (Greg is banned from saying when he's coming) and listen to what they say.

Feel tired but hopeful as I go down to the Cottesloe. The route is all very familiar – the stairs, the swing doors, the backstage dock – from *Stanley*, *Titus*, *Vanya*, all the way back to *True West*. It's all very familiar, and this lifts the heart.

The dress rehearsal goes well. I'm a bit nervous to start with, but this passes, and then I just get more and more at ease, until I'm virtually enjoying it. The odd little stumble over lines still gives me a bad fright. But if ever there was a show to practise Greg's advice about mid-show blunders – *don't carry the baggage* – it's this one. If you carry the baggage (ie. thinking about the blunder while moving on) you'll just create another trip-up, and possibly a worse accident. The other vital note from tonight is: *drink calmly*. I drank too greedily during one water-stop, and had a slight coughing fit.

We'd decided on no audience for the dress – we'd just do it for ourselves – but neverthelss some people who're working on the show sat in, and when it's over, the best compliment comes from the most surprising source. My dresser, Ali Blandford, is in tears. She's a tough London gal, who's worked at Stratford East for years before coming here, so she's no push-over – yet she's very cut up as we go up the stairs. Keeps apologising and taking deep breaths. Back in the dressing-room, I pour her a big glass of Chablis. She sobs: 'But I should be doing that for you!'

Richard comes in – very pleased. He actually compliments me: 'You were wonderful.' (Normally he'll just say, rather guardedly, 'Yes that was fine'.) He also mentions that Hildegard sends much praise.

After he's gone, I find her in the green room. We have a drink, and then share a taxi north. Turns out she shares my unease with Richard's fiercely controlling hand. I urge her to sit him down tomorrow, and talk through any worries. I feel sure he won't dismiss her as cursorily as he sometimes does me (bought on friendship's ticket). We agree that Richard is doing a fine job on this – the whole of Auschwitz is on stage even although nothing is actually there – but that doesn't mean he can't also be wrong from time to time. We end the discussion with laughter, remembering how, if Richard had his way, Primo would be wearing a Fair Isle sweater and brogues.

Friday 24th September 2004

Dear Primo,

Woke on this, the day of our first preview, our first public performance, with a most unique feeling. No nerves. That's never happened before.

Before Greg left for work, he gave me a hug and said, 'Enjoy tonight.' I said, 'Oh I thought you were wishing me Yom Kippur.' He said, 'OK – have a happy Yom Kippur.' I said, 'I don't think one says that.' He said, 'OK – have an unhappy Yom Kippur.'

Then he went. I'm going in now. Wish me well.

With love,

Tony.

At 2.30 pm we did our second dress. Quite a sizeable audience: it was open to anyone working in the building. No onset of The Fear, although I noticed that when I went near the edge of the stage in the early sections – which are tense anyway (the train journey, the arrival) and very dark – a tiny tremor started in my legs. It was odd. My top half was calm – voice steady, no drying of the mouth – my lower half was tense. Afterwards, I asked Richard if this showed? He said not. But also said the run wasn't as good as last night. I didn't really care. I'm doing my best.

Hours to fill before the first preview. Began to feel the loneliness of the one-man show. Munched on half a sandwich (can't really eat before a show), read the David Hare book, had a delicious doze, one of those where you dip under, go deep, then surface again. Went down to the stage and wandered around, reminding myself of the sequence of the episodes (still my greatest worry) and of Richard's specific notes (it's always best to revise notes in situ).

Felt remarkably calm as the performance approached, smiling at the absurdity of the tannoy calls:

'*Funny Thing* – cast, crew, revolve operator, orchestra.'

'*Buried Child* – cast, crew, musicians.'

'*Primo* – Mr Sher.'

Took a final breath of strength, laying my hands on my Primo talisman, which I keep locked in my dressing-table drawer: his school report, with 10 out of 10 for Good Behaviour, and the 3 Auschwitz stones, all these placed on a small glass tray which Greg gave me as an early first-night present. Then I strolled downstairs rather breezily. I've always believed that a leading actor should try to emanate a sense of relaxation backstage; it's part of his job, something he shares with the director; it makes the rest of the cast feel they're on a steady ship. Since there's no rest of the cast on this, I resolved to chat with anyone I met. It's a curious double bluff: if you pretend to be OK, you don't only make them feel OK, you make yourself feel OK.

The first person I saw in the back-dock was Production Manager Jason Barnes. We've been friends for years. He's a veteran of the NT, a real theatre enthusiast. Usually wears jeans with braces. Tonight, I was surprised to see him in jacket and tie. He said he'd come straight from the funeral of Andy Phillips, the renowned Lighting Designer. Then added:

'I've just told Greg the same thing.'

I went still. 'What?'

He said it again, cheerfully – 'Greg' – pointing front-of-house.

I said quietly, 'I didn't know Greg was in.'

It was his turn to go still. I don't know which one of us was more shocked.

I ended up reassuring him that it didn't matter. And it didn't actually. There's something so enormous about this task that routine theatre worries like 'who's in' cease to matter.

Ernie was also in the back-dock, wearing his cans (headphones). He got the stand-by from Thomas – in his booth at the back of the auditorium – and then accompanied me down to a little air-lock directly behind the set. The Cottesloe is like the Swan: it has no wings – before entrances, you wait in airlocks or gangways. Ernie and I stood in the dark, chatting. The feeling was like waiting to see the doctor, with a favourite uncle at your side. On the wall, a red light went on. Ernie took hold of the door handle. I moved next to it. From the auditorium, I heard the announcement about mobile phones. Half-heard, through Ernie's cans, Thomas giving the opening cues. Saw the pre-set lights dim to blackout. The first cello piece started, the red light changed to green, and Ernie opened the door. I stepped through, found my mark on the floor – in luminous tape – and the lights came up, revealing me at the very back of the set. I took a deep breath, said inwardly, 'This is for Primo', and walked forward.

It was a jolt to see the auditorium packed to the rafters. I spoke the first line – 'It was my good fortune to be deported to

Auschwitz only in 1944' – and I was off, with the awareness that I wouldn't stop speaking for another hour and a half. There was no onset of The Fear, though I did notice that a part of me was ticking off the sections, wanting it to be over. It was so unfamiliar again, like the first run in the rehearsal room, and the beginning of the tech, and the dress. This show is playing a weird board game with me, where I keep being sent back to Square One. It's like when Primo's discharged from the infirmary, and talks about leaving naked again, trying to adapt very quickly, just like at the beginning.

Well, tonight I got to the end, back to my opening position, but now facing the wall. The lights went down, the last cello piece finished, and I saw Ernie open the door for me. I went into the air-lock. Here I was suddenly overcome, and lent on a table, shaken by sobs. I was aware that Ernie was standing alongside, unsure what to do, so I quickly got myself together. We had decided to try taking no curtain call (as I'd written in the script). They didn't clap at first, then they did. The house lights came up. They carried on. I said to Ernie: 'I'd better go out and do a bow.' He relayed this to Thomas, who changed the lights again. I stepped through the door, and was about to turn the corner onto the set when the applause finally finished. I darted back to Ernie. Some of the audience must've seen half my sleeve.

Met Richard on the stairs. He was grinning and happy, and embraced me. I said, 'Careful, the grey from my beard comes off.' He said, 'Oh sod the grey from your beard – well done! – you did splendidly! – and the buzz on this is wonderful, *wonderful* .' He came with me to the dressing room, where Ali was waiting with a chilled bottle of Chablis. As I changed out of my costume, I noticed my shirt was dry. I hadn't sweated at all. That's never happened in a show before. I said to Richard, 'Your crazy note worked!'

We were toasting one another when Greg walked in. He was in tears, and hugged me, then Richard. I said, 'Look at the state of you.' He said, 'Maybe it was just seeing you get through it.'

And that's when I sensed something wasn't quite right. I wondered if maybe he hadn't bought it – the way we're doing the show.

When we were left alone, I pre-empted things by suggesting that he give any notes to Richard, not me. This is a traditional theatre courtesy. If you're in preview, and if your partner comes along (even if they're not a director themselves), it's good manners to let their comments be filtered through the director of the show. He or she has got to be your first point of contact.

In the bar Richard and Greg chatted to one side, while I talked to the other people who'd been in: Pádraig Cusack, Jack Bradley, the actors Bill Paterson (Hildegard's partner) and David Tennant. Everyone was full of encouragement, but felt I should take a curtain call. After tonight, it's obvious that I should, and will. But it's a pity. If the show works *exactly* as it should, people wouldn't be able to clap. Or is it just British politeness? Or just theatre tradition – impossible to break? Richard and Greg finished their talk (neither looked perturbed, so I decided Greg's reservations couldn't be too serious) and joined our group. Richard was drinking tonight – he's usually very abstemious – and happier, laughier than I've seen him in ages. My old friend was back. I realised that I've missed him. And also that I keep forgetting he's nervous too, and how much is at stake for him: as a director, this show is his National Theatre debut.

In the car home, Greg said that Richard had 'given permission' for him to tell me what he thought. As I might have predicted, Greg felt the whole experience was slightly emotionally cool. He wanted Primo to lose his calm, his analytical, scientist's calm, on a couple of occasions: after the chemistry exam, on 'I judge you', and after the selection, on 'If I was God I would spit at God's prayer.' And although he was moved by the death of Alberto, he didn't understand why I was covering up my feelings so fiercely (I'm still battling real tears here,

every time). He thought that moments of fury and grief would
shock the audience, and make them realise how much Primo
was holding inside. These outbursts would earn all the steadi-
ness elsewhere. This confirmed something I'd often worried
about: the same-iness of my performance.

Dear Primo,
    Back at home. Angry. With myself mostly. For not con-
fronting Richard more. I've never fought for what I
believed, what I felt. And I've always felt there should be
more feeling. But Richard's dead against this. I've given
him the benefit of the doubt, because his overall concept
for the show and indeed the character has been inspira-
tional. But what if he's wrong about this one crucial area?
Wrong but immovable, as is his way. The trouble with
directors who have a strict and singular Theory of Acting
is that we learn from them, but do they ever learn from
us? I mean, I'm not complete rubbish as an actor. If rehearsals had been more open – Richard's favourite word –
he might have been surprised and interested by some of my
insights, or perhaps more importantly my feelings. Instead
every time he says I should 'Primo-tize' it more, I just
hear him saying 'Richard-ize' it more. Richard has complete control over himself, cast-iron control, in that fearsome Scottish way – I've known him closely for thirty
years, yet never once seen him cry or heard him ask for
help.
    I don't think that you were like that. Could you have
been a depressive, could you have committed suicide if
you were like that? Maybe – by holding it all in, and then
finding it explodes. I don't know.
    Am I playing you wrong. Am I?
    I wish you could answer.
    With love,
    Tony.

Saturday 25th September 2004

Hang on, I said it too casually yesterday – 'There was no onset of The Fear'. Hang on, this was a more important moment. This was my first public performance since *Othello* and there was no Fear. I've done it – I've cracked it. THERE WAS NO FUCKING FEAR. That's thanks to those letters to Primo, and that one word again and again: love, love, love. And as Greg said: *Primo* is too important for The Fear.

But even while celebrating this, I felt tired and edgy. Greg's notes were weighing heavy on me. At the end of our discussion last night, we concluded that maybe Richard thought the notes were valid – otherwise why let Greg tell me? I resolved to discuss them with Richard when the right moment arose . . .

This afternoon, we ran some sequences for our production photographer, Ivan Kyncl: Czech, stocky, red-haired, bearded. *Primo* suddenly turned into a two-man show, for Ivan clambered on stage, and followed me round, shooting from every possible angle. This would have been intolerable if it were not for two things: Ivan and I have been friends for a long time, and I knew the results would be good. This show is right up his street. He was a political prisoner himself, in his homeland, with Vaclav Havel. His photographic style is brutal and beautiful, exactly right for us. But his methods are unusual, to say the least. He shoots like a war correspondent, scurrying round between the action, dashing in to grab this or that angle, sweating and concentrated. This went on even after his session was over. We told him we had to continue with our work. He retreated to the side of the stage, but stayed there, alert and hopeful, like a pet dog at a dining-room table, and when any opportunity arose he darted over to me again and started clicking away, desperate for just one more angle, one more shot – maybe the prize shot. I love him. We call him Ivan the Terrible, while knowing he's actually Ivan the Great.

Two major changes happened during the work session, and in a show as minimalist as this, any change is major. Firstly, the chair was replaced with a different one: the chair which I've worked with for six weeks now, and which has become not only Dr Pannwitz, Ka-Be, and the gallows, but something of a friend. Secondly, I lost my centre mark: a small piece of white tape on the front of the stage, which helps me locate myself for certain key positions. But it shows up against the lead floor, and has been driving both Hildegard and Richard mad. So it was ripped off now, and replaced with a red eye – a light – at the back of the auditorium, in line with the centre of the stage. I would have to spend the rest of the afternoon adjusting to it.

At last – they didn't need me for the next cue, and Richard didn't seem occupied either – at last my moment had come. I climbed down into the auditorium, and sought him out:

'With regard to Greg's notes, I'd like to – '

He interrupted instantly: 'Of course I don't necessarily agree with them!'

I replied calmly: 'No, but since you let him give them to me, I'd like to address them.'

I said I'd like to try some slightly different things in the evening's performance – emphasising *slightly* – and I didn't want to discuss these till afterwards; I didn't want to feel self-conscious when I came to those moments in the show. As I spoke, Richard began radiating impatience and immovability. This is one of his less impressive qualities as a director: when in disagreement with you, he'll barely listen, he'll just make you feel like an idiot, wasting his time. I persisted: this was a preview, and previews are a time to *try* things. He said OK in a way that meant it wasn't OK, and I walked away hating him (for a moment).

Up in my dressing room, I was getting into a right state when, luckily, Greg rang from Wales (where the family are meeting this weekend). He said that, when we discussed his reaction to the show last night, we'd focused too much on his reservations, which were only minor anyway, only a matter of degree. Overall, he thought the production and my performance were very moving – we'd seen his tears when he came into the dressing room. He said the restraint was good, more than good. I was doing acting that he'd never seen me do before (which is quite a statement coming from him), and it's entirely thanks to Richard. So I shouldn't get too angry with him.

As I put down the phone I realised that Richard is also partly responsible for the disappearance of my stage fright. Even though he's never actually known about it, he somehow switched my attention from any actory neurosis, or vanity, to the total importance of the character, of Primo. In a way, Richard simply banned The Fear, like he banned sweating. So there is an up-side to absolute rule.

Feeling better now, I prepared for the show.

Just before it started, when Ernie and I were waiting in the air-lock, I suddenly became anxious about my red light – my new centre-stage marker. Ernie said he's already checked it, but would do so again, and spoke to Thomas through his mouth piece. The message came back that yes it was on. The cue came to start, I walked out, and the first thing I noticed was – no red light.

Now what do I do? I never go offstage. There's no opportunity, as there would be in an ordinary show, to whisper to another actor, and get the word to stage management that there's a problem. Instead I had an hour and a half ahead of dealing with it myself.

This made me so angry I became completely calm, and did the show rather well, I thought, with real emotion flashing through on the moments of fury and grief. Then, in the last quarter of the show, the red light suddenly came on.

At the end, after I'd taken our new curtain call, I asked Ernie to investigate. He checked with the lighting box, then apologised on behalf of everyone. Because the red light was inserted halfway through this afternoon's work it became linked to a specific lighting cue, accidentally, and couldn't function on its own. This would be rectified.

Richard came round to the dressing room, bringing along Patsy Rodenburg and her partner, the dancer Antonia Francesci.

Richard said my performance was a bit down tonight. Patsy agreed – even vocally it was a bit down. I felt indifferent to their comments. There's something about this show that sweeps away the negative emotions which can sometimes oppress actors: nerves beforehand, disappointment afterwards. And anyway, Antonia, who had nothing to compare it with, was knocked out by the show. Said it was very moving. Patsy said the 'I judge you' line was electric. I asked Richard what he thought about these stronger moments of emotion. He said he wasn't at all sure about them. I decided not to pursue the subject for now.

Sunday 26th September 2004

I must confront the situation with Richard. Basically, we're working together really well – the reactions to the show are better than either of us could've hoped – and there are only two small areas of disagreement: the moments of emotion, and an occasional busy-ness to Paul's otherwise excellent lighting. I would write Richard a fax. That way I wouldn't have to suffer his impatience, and he'd have to at least consider my point of view. I wrote it carefully, asking him to be *open* – 'this is something you sometimes preach more than practise' – and saying yes, I was giving him a note, and please could he take it. Then I faxed it to him, and began holding my breath.

I lunched at the Almeida Restaurant with my South African pal and *Othello* co-star, Sello. We were there for hours – so much to catch up on. He'd applied for the Artistic Directorship of Jo'burg's Market Theatre, but didn't get it, and is now doing a screenwriter's course at Leeds University. Wants to go back to South Africa, and make films. Excellent. I'm all for people spreading their wings, changing careers or pursuing more than one. I also reminded Sello that ever since Greg *didn't* get the job of running the RSC, his career has gone on an upward trajectory. Something was liberated – in him and the profession, even among the critics.

By the time I got home, Greg was back. When I told him about the fax to Richard, he roared with laughter. 'Richard's been faxed! I must tell him what a compliment this is. All of Tony's directors get faxed at some stage or another. Once you even faxed *me*.'

Soon after, Richard rang. Sounded relaxed and warm. Said yes of course we must meet and discuss these differences.

Monday 27th September 2004

Today, as agreed, Richard and I meet for lunch in the National canteen. And it is, as I requested, completely *open*. We discuss a good compromise for the end of the *Selekcja* section, when Primo says, 'If I was God, I would spit at Kuhn's prayer.' At the moment, I'm very far upstage. Yet for all the other 'important' moments in the piece, I go downstage, to the very edge, almost breaking through Theatre's fourth wall. We'll re-block this moment, bringing me to the downstage position. In return, I'll keep it (relatively) restrained. I'm happy with this, because what Richard maybe doesn't realise is that there's already enormous emotion going on internally, but the audience just can't see it – can't see my eyes, can't see inside my head. In fact, I agree with him about actors emoting too much. (Olivier once said of an actress he was working with: 'She keeps trying to cry. In real life, we try *not* to cry.') With regard to the busy-ness of the lighting, Richard says he and Paul have already agreed to reduce this: the green is being cut completely from the meadow sequence, and the red is being lessened in the bombed camp.

Afterwards I thank Richard for his openness, and for 'taking the note', a phrase which directors normally use with argumentative actors: 'Please just take the note!'

At the beginning of this afternoon's work, we do a good exercise to help me grasp the acoustics of the auditorium: Richard stands on stage speaking (he's a very funny raconteur, and the

technical team are in stitches), while I move round the different levels, listening to him. The Cottesloe is bigger than one
thinks. When I get back onstage, and give it a bit more volume, a
bit more breath (on Patsy's advice), it immediately feels better.

Tonight is one of those gala nights – a charity has bought
out the house – and these are always difficult, always less
focused. The audience is made up of rich people rather than
theatre-buffs. The motivation is different: they're driven by a
desire to support the charity rather than see the show, and may
have no real interest in it.

At one point I hear a prolonged kerfuffle going on in the
auditorium, and afterwards discover that a man fainted and
had to be carried out. While he was being given first-aid in the
foyer, his wife said to the St John's man: 'He's always doing this
if it's a Holocaust thing – we were watching a telly programme
on it the other day, and he did it then!' We wondered why they
came. (Probably just for the charity.) The wife had a further
problem: she'd kicked off her shoes as the show started, and
could she just tiptoe back in to fetch them? She was told
absolutely not. Although I'm not driven to distraction by
coughers – like David Hare (and, according to him, Kevin
Spacey) – I'm nevertheless amazed by the insensitivity of some
audience members. On Saturday night when I was talking about
the Auschwitz hunger – 'It's unknown to free men' – a man in
the front row started to dig noisily in a bag of sweets.

Tonight's incident also reminds me of that *Othello* performance in the Swan when a man fainted during the Senate
scene. Iago is standing silently at the back throughout, so I was
able to watch. The surrounding audience members – being
British and polite – began to whisper, 'Is there a doctor in the
house?' The man's wife whispered back: 'He *is* a doctor.'

Dear Primo,
    James Thompson, the trauma psychiatrist who visited
our workshop, and his wife (also a psychiatrist) were in

tonight. Richard and I had a drink with them in the green room afterwards. It was good to hear their very positive reactions. I was particularly pleased when Mrs Thompson said, 'I felt you were speaking just to me.'

I told James how much I valued the essay by you that he sent me. On the subject of Kafka. Containing an unexpected but wonderful message. Discussing why you admire Kafka but don't like him, you say that his writing always looks into the dark, while yours looks into the light.

This from you . . . ?

It's helped me.

With love,

Tony.

Tuesday 28th September 2004

Bad dreams again, so went to my Marietta session in a rather jumpy state, and came out an hour later feeling on top of the world. We discussed the little leg tremor which still afflicts me in the early part of the show when I'm close to the edge of the stage and surrounded by darkness. She said, 'Is it manageable?' I replied chirpily, 'Oh yes.' She said, 'Well, isn't that OK then? If tension has come out somewhere, isn't it good that it's somewhere no-one can see?' I said, 'You mean, down my trouser leg?' She said, 'Exactly,' and we laughed. Afterwards, I thought how remarkably adaptable the human mind is. In recent years, I've been tormented by an inner demon, nicknamed The Fear. It's unacceptable for this show – it would make it impossible to do. Yet I have to do it. I've fought long and hard to do it. So somehow The Fear has turned into just a tiny shiver in the leg.

Following this excellent Marietta session, I had an excellent Patsy session. In the Cottesloe, just on our own. I told Patsy how pleased I was by James Thompson's wife saying she felt I was just talking to her. Patsy said, 'Good, just talk to me then'

– and then went to stand in the furthest corners of the upper levels. Two important developments: 1. I got the measure of the space; 2. I started speaking instead of declaiming.

In the technical session that followed, I noticed they had the new version of the slide which comes up at the end, of Primo himself. I had suggested this slide some time ago, hoping it could substitute for the curtain call. Now we do both. They've had technical problems with the image and it's been rather blurred. Today it was clear. So I finally saw it, and realised they'd got his death date wrong: '86 instead of '87. They're going to correct it, but in a way I'd prefer there to be no mention of his dates at all. It somehow brings his death into the picture, and, as I discovered in that first clumsy draft of the script, the subject is out of place. On the other hand, as Richard said, 'The audience should know he lived for forty years after Auschwitz.' I'm not going into battle over this one.

Tonight's show was good. Both of today's solo sessions – with Marietta and with Patsy – paid off. I was more relaxed, and felt I was talking more naturally: stringing words together in a flow, rather than proceeding from one to the next with a mixture of precision and caution, as though negotiating stepping stones. At the end, there was no applause, which thrilled me – till some dork started it. Turned out to be Richard.

(Well . . . I know that directors sometimes do this . . . I've sat next to Greg at previews.)

Richard and I have been wondering why Nick H. has left us alone for so long. He was on holiday during our rehearsal runs and the first previews, but he was back yesterday – yet didn't come to see us. (Turns out he went to *Buried Child* instead, which opens first, tomorrow night.) Tonight, he walked into the dressing room. Glowing with praise and pride. Kept saying 'Thank you' to both of us. Richard invited him to give notes. He said he didn't have any. Found the restraint perfectly judged; what he called the refusal 'to ask for cheap tears'.

Once again it's being confirmed: Richard's take on this piece is *right*.

Wednesday 29th September 2004

Took one-and-a-half sleeping pills, yet still woke very early, after this dream:

Greg and I walk through empty car parks and shopping precincts, then suddenly emerge onto the brim of a spectacular African landscape, like the Ngorogoro Crater in Tanzania (where we Christmassed with Richard in 2003). People are sitting around, relaxing with sundowners, although there are pythons between their feet. A small antelope charges me. I grab it and throw it aside. Everyone else leaves. Greg and I are alone in the bush. We feel we'll survive here. We'll start by trying to kill something . . .

At first I feel disturbed by the dream . . . then realise it holds some beauty and hope . . .

I'm still doing my countdown. *Today is Wednesday – which is better than Thursday.*

I've been given the morning off again. Spend it writing first-night cards – with my drawing of Primo and self sprinting forward – this will take the pressure off tomorrow.

In the afternoon, we did a photo call for the press, and then worked on bits and pieces. Richard was so relaxed by now he sloped off to do a fencing class for a scene in his new telly series, *Born and Bred* – he films it on Friday, the day after we open – while Paul and the lighting team tinkered with this and that, and I wandered around the stage doing sections.

In the early evening, when I popped down to fetch something from the stage door, I saw that two trestle tables had been set up there, and that these were laden with flowers, champagne and cards. It's the press night of *Buried Child*. Members of the cast were collecting their gifts, including the American

actress Lauren Ambrose. I'm rather in awe of her. Her TV
series *Six Feet Under* has been one of the best things on the box
in recent years, and her performance as the disturbed daughter
is, well, disturbing. In real life she's a calm and easy presence.
She asked me when *Primo* opens. I said, 'Well, we go through
all of this tomorrow.' She laughed: 'Who's *we*, Tonto?'

Tonight's show was good, the audience exceptionally still.
Afterwards, Richard came into the dressing room, and said,
'I've got only one note for you, and here it is' – tore a page from
his notebook, and handed it over. In big letters he'd scrawled,
'Pure Primo – brilliant.' After all his relentless and rigorous
criticism, this was very touching. After he'd gone, I added it to
my Primo talisman in the dressing-table drawer. Then I went
to the bar, and found several friends there: the television producer Robert Marshall (in tears), the publisher Nick Hern and
his partner, the actress Jane Maud – all very enthusiastic.

Dear Primo,
   At home, I switched on the telly, to see Ken Bigley
(the British hostage in Iraq), chained, in a cage, pleading
with Blair: 'Please . . . I don't want to die . . . please help
me . . . '. I switched channels. I have to turn away from
this story. It's too painful at the moment. Too close,
somehow. Someone trying to survive. With even less
chance, I think, than you had.
   And so, into tomorrow . . .
   With love,
   Tony.

Thursday 30th September 2004

Dear Primo,
   Woke at 7, having taken two Temazepan, and having had
a good solid sleep. Don't think I even went for a pee in the

night. First thought – it's today. Second thought – there's no fear. I can't tell you how unique this is.

After Greg left for work, I opened his card. He said that it wasn't only my performance and adaptation that moves him, but 'the respect for your subject, the care for it, love for it, for him, for Primo'. I sat in the kitchen crying, peacefully.

I'm so glad I requested a matinee today. People thought I was crazy, but I knew from experience (I think the first time was *Tamburlaine*) that a matinee before opening night is just what the doctor ordered. By the time the evening show comes, you just feel like all actors do on matinee days: bit tired, bit bored, bit pissed off. Perfect. Now you stand a chance of achieving that state which makes for good acting: a balance between concentration and relaxation. Often on press nights, actors are over-concentrated and under-relaxed.

11.30am. I'm going to the theatre now.

When next I write to you it will be with good news.

With love,

Tony.

The matinee is the worst show yet. Richard isn't in, so I don't have his ferocious eagle eye aimed at me. I decide I'll take it very easy, won't even do the lines beforehand. This is a mistake. Early on, during the train journey, I get a fright:

'Through the air-slit, we saw the tall pale cliffs of the Adige . . . '

Adige what? Adige Valley? No, it can't be a valley, how could a valley be tall? Just say valley . . .

' . . . Valley.'

Actually, I think valley is right.

From then on, I'm very nervous. The leg tremble is almost unbearable.

I'm going to fall off the stage . . . !

Now external forces descend as well. During the Pannwitz exam, I hear strange, regular knocking. It doesn't stop.

Is it a member of the audience . . . some kind of protest? What the fuck is going on?

After a couple of minutes it fades, then vanishes. When eventually the show finishes, Ernie apologises. Apparently it was some engineers working on the Olivier drum revolve. He stopped them as soon as he realised, and will be submitting a complaint in the show report.

Back in the dressing room, I sit staring at myself in the mirror. *What happened this afternoon? Was that a return of The Fear? Now? Of all times . . . ? No. I won't let it be. I will not let it back in.*

I immediately feel stronger. Three hours to curtain-up. They pass very quickly, in a kind of blur. Beautiful bunches of flowers keep arriving, bottles of champagne, presents and cards. My dressing room gradually transforms itself into a florist/off-licence/gift shop. Richard gives me a fine leather notebook embossed with 174517, Primo's number. I give him a glowing piece of amber bought in Kraków. Our cards to one another both register the same thing: *Primo* is a monument to our friendship. Ali's present is lovely, right up my street: some little stones from the Valley of the Kings in Egypt. Jonathan's is a framed sheet of music: my favourite piece from the show – Primo's theme. Tremendous messages on cards, from Nick H., Pádraig, Hildegard, Paul, many others, and a fax from the family at home, saying they'll be onstage with me in spirit. What with Primo as well, and Michael Bryant's ghost, it's going to be pretty crowded out there tonight.

6.45pm. Richard has already wished me well, but I bump into him in the Gents, and tell him something important I've just remembered, and which is going to clinch things for me. At one point in their friendship, Primo (who was weak and clumsy) asked Alberto (who was strong and resourceful) why he bothered with him. Alberto replied, 'Because you carry luck.'

7pm. I feel calm. As soon as the show starts, I know I'm going to be fine: there's no leg shiver. This afternoon's matinee has paid off: both because I've done the show once already, and because it wasn't very good. I had feared I might spot the critics scribbling away and this might distract me, but I don't even glimpse them. The stillness of tonight's audience is remarkable. They treat the piece as though it's music, listening with rapt attention, only coughing or clearing their throats inbetween the movements; i.e. during the little blackouts. And then a terrific thing happens at the end. No-one claps. For a long time. It's a great compliment, that silence. Spoiled only, and hilariously, by Ernie as I come off. Instead of handing me my usual glass of water, he's prepared a G & T. He apologises that there's no slice of lemon – forgetting that the door is still open, and the audience stock-still. So tonight, for the first few rows at least, Primo's epic story of survival finishes with this line: 'Sorry there's no lemon'.

Then they begin clapping.

Up in the dressing room, I know I've acquitted myself well – even before Richard comes in, grinning broadly, followed by Greg, his sister Jo, and my agent Paul Lyon-Maris, all full of praise.

At the party in the Cottesloe foyer, there's a big crowd, including Nick H., Pádraig, Bill Paterson again, Richard's chum Angus Deayton, my other agent Mic and her son Olly – she hugs me and whispers, 'We got there!' – and some surprise visitors from Italy: Roberto Gilodi, also Primo's English translator, Stuart Woolf, and his wife. Both Roberto and Stuart are very moved, and could not be more complimentary. I glow with relief. This will go straight back to Primo's family. Stuart's wife, Anna, is Italian and reveals that she is the niece of Primo's other devoted soul-mate in Auschwitz, Leonardo De Benedetti. I apologise for the fact that I've cut him completely from the story. It was one of the painful sacrifices when I was struggling to reduce the book down to our playing time.

She says she doesn't mind. All three of them feel I've abridged the book with complete sensitivity.

We invite them to join us for dinner in the National's restaurant, the Mezzanine. I sit between Stuart and Anna. He tells me that he translated *If This Is A Man* together with Primo himself – I never realised this – working in the study at 75 Corso Re Umberto, once a week, starting at 9pm, after Primo got back from work at the SIVA factory and had finished dinner. He also reveals that Primo was a conscientious file-keeper, and that when Lucia passes away there'll be a lot of extra material about him – letters and so on – if Renzo and Lisa will ever allow this to be published. I try to discuss the suicide with Stuart, but he can't – says it's still too upsetting. All he says is: 'It wasn't an accident – the balustrade is too high.' Anna talks, touchingly, of Primo's friendship with her uncle, which continued for the rest of Primo's life: Leonardo lived very close, Primo visted all the time, Anna often met him there.

And so this monumental day ends in a most unexpected and pleasing way: surrounded not only by my nearest and dearest, but a group of people who knew Primo well, and have seen the show, and liked it. When I first wrote it, back in November 2002, could I ever have dreamed of this dinner party?

Primo says that in Auschwitz they needed a new language, with new words, to adequately describe 'hunger' and 'cold'. I need a new one for 'relief'.

Friday 1st October 2004

Dear Primo,

I said I'd report back with good news, and I can. The press night went well, the reviews are raves (when Greg and Paul Lyon-Maris marked them out of ten, we got the same score as you did for Good Behaviour), and Nick H. has already phoned to discuss a further run after South Africa. Best of all, I don't have another performance till

next Thursday, so Greg and I are off to Stratford, which
is probably my second favourite place on earth – after
Cape Town.
    With love,
    Tony.

Sunday 3rd October 2004

Dear Primo,
    This correspondence must come to an end. I can't
spend the rest of my life writing to you. Greg and I are
staying at one of the hotels we return to again and again,
Mallory Court, near Leamington. Apart from its excellent
food, rooms, and views, another of its appeals is that it's
near to the Inigo Jones windmill which stands on that hill
through the window, just over there, overlooking fields.
One of these used to be a cornfield – it's now sliced through
by the M40 motorway. Before this was constructed, Greg
and I once had a picnic in that cornfield. This was in 1987.
The year you died. The year our relationship began. We
were both actors at the RSC then; I was doing *Merchant*
and *Revenger's Tragedy*. That summer was the worst on
record. The cricket commentator, Brian Johnston, said it
was a *Madame Butterfly* summer – there was only 'one
fine day'. On that day, a Sunday, we drove to the windmill,
found a secluded corner of the cornfield, took off our
clothes and had a glorious morning and afternoon in the
sun. One fine day. Today's also a fine day. The Sunday
reviews have kept the score at full marks. When Richard
and I spoke on the phone we were both more stunned
than pleased. Every time you do a show you dream of this
result, but it very rarely happens. Greg and I celebrated
with a superb dinner in the restaurant here, though a very
early dinner – while trawling through all the Sunday papers
this morning, Greg noticed there was a programme about

lions at 8.30. Watching wildlife programmes – and indeed going on wildlife safaris – are among our most cherished pastimes. I said, 'A programme about lions? To finish this particular week? Primo was wrong – there is a God.'

I'm signing off now.

Thank you.

With love,

Tony.

Tuesday 9th November 2004

Five weeks later . . .

This morning my brother Randall rings from Cape Town, sounding very excited. He says, 'You're on all the lamp-posts here!' I say, 'What, you mean posters of *Primo* for the Baxter run?' He says, 'No, it's this morning's Cape Times – you know those boards that newspapers do with the headlines? – well, this one says "Antony Sher To Act In City" – it's on all the lamp-posts!'

The news of the Baxter run has clearly just been announced back home. I tell Randall that I was amazed last night when Mom rang. She hasn't rung for years. (I normally ring her.) But she'd just seen an article in the Cape Argus about *Primo* at the Baxter, and, although she's often been told about this, it hadn't really registered till now: in black and white, in the evening paper. She was beside herself with joy – 'I can't eat, I won't sleep!' – sounding like she used to, the Jewish Mother getting *naches* from her son's achievements; as opposed to the Jewish Mother telling everyone that, shame, her son is a failed actor in England. It was very touching. She said, 'I'm counting the days.' I said, 'Me too.' She was re-energised. When we'd spoken previously, she'd said rather vaguely, 'Give my love to everyone there.' Last night she said, 'Give my love to Greg.'

Thinking it through, I realise that the Cape Town run will include Holocaust Day, the 27th of January, and that it will be

a special anniversary: sixty years since the liberation of Auschwitz by the Russians. On that night in Cape Town, what will it
feel like to describe this at the end of *Primo*? The arrival of the
four Russian soldiers - 'four messengers of peace'. The people at
the Baxter say that Desmond Tutu will attend that performance.

In London the show is a success. The letters I'm receiving
are unlike any I've ever known: they don't talk about the acting
or writing, they don't talk about theatre really; they talk about
Primo Levi, they talk about going through Auschwitz with
him. The Sunday Times and several other papers have made
Primo their number one choice of theatre to see. Trouble is,
you can't get tickets for it. Even the secret box office allo-
cations, including my own, are gone. We're bringing it back
after South Africa – for a straight run at Hampstead Theatre.
I've agreed to 6 performances a week for 4 weeks. What will
that be like? Probably easier than the broken patterns of performance in the National's repertoire. (Each time I go back after
a break, it's also back to that cruel board game, back to Square
One.) There's talk of New York too, and possibly a TV film.
And I've been commissioned by Nick Hern to write a book –
this book – about the whole experience. My journey is starting
to ape David Hare's, except that he did hundreds of performances, in the West End, on Broadway, and currently he's doing
it *again*, in Australia for God's sake! The man's either tougher
or madder than I am.

I write to him, praising *Acting Up*. He writes back, saying
that he regards the book as a failure. He meant it as a discussion
about acting for people outside the business. Instead, it seems
to have just served as a security blanket for neurotic old pros
like me.

Stuart Woolf sends me a fascinating essay of his: *Primo Levi's
Sense Of History*. At one point he quotes Primo from *Conver-
sazioni* (Einaudi, 1985), and it's like the man himself confirming
that we're doing the show correctly: 'It is more effective to
witness with restraint rather than anger.' I don't show this to

Richard. He's been proved right too often; it's not good for him.

It's one of those extraordinary times when extraordinary things happen.

A week after photographing our show, Ivan Kyncl died. Impossible. He was as strong as an ox. He'd been a political prisoner in Czechoslovakia, an asylum seeker in London, living rough on the streets. You couldn't kill him. What, no more Ivan – darting between the action like a war correspondent? No more Ivan the Terrible – actually, Ivan the Great? Impossible.

And then on one *Primo* night I heard that Trude Levi was in. Trude, the 80-year-old survivor of the Buchenwald slave camp, Hessisch-Lichtenau, the survivor who'd visited the Studio workshop and inspired our way of playing *Primo*. I wondered if she'd come round to see me afterwards. She didn't. Maybe she didn't know she could, or maybe the show offended her. I was hurrying through the main house foyer afterwards, on the way to meet friends in the restaurant, when I saw her sitting there, her stick at her side, waiting for a taxi. I wasn't sure whether to say hello. Then she saw me, and reached out. I took her hand, and knelt next to her. She said, 'Thank you.' She was clearly very moved. And very different to the woman who'd come to the workshop. That one was, in Richard's rough phrase, 'tough as old boots'. This one was smaller, younger, much more vulnerable. *Primo* had taken her back, I think, to things she'd experienced in 1944. She said she was particularly touched by my composure. I said, 'But Trude – that all comes from you – you showed us how to do it.' Her eyes filled again. We stayed there, both emotional, both saying thank you to one another. It was a moment I won't forget.

But the most extraordinary thing in this extraordinary time is the letter which comes with this morning's post. It's from Italy, from Turin, and written on the envelope is this name and address: Levi, 75 Corso Re Umberto. I stare at it, frowning. For a fleeting moment I think that Primo has written to me, replying at last to all my letters. My hand trembles as I tear open the flap. There's a single typed page inside, signed in pen: Renzo. Primo's son. This is my first direct contact with the Levi family. In the past, I've often felt mystified and frustated by their behaviour, I've felt them standing between me and Primo, and I've sometimes wanted to yell: He's ours as well as yours. But I feel differently now, probably because there's no longer a struggle. They're obviously intensely private people, and they're forced to carry the weight of both Primo's Auschwitz experience (which they remember not as words in a famous book, but a tattoo on their father's arm) and of his violent death. How do I know what that's like?

After the first night of *Primo*, both Roberto and Stuart relayed their impressions to the family, and then Stuart encouraged me to contact Renzo. I wrote to him. (This letter went through more drafts than the script.) There was silence for several weeks. And now finally today's reply.

Renzo apologises for what he calls a moment of shyness when we were in Turin. He intended to come and see us at the Department of Chemistry, but changed his mind at the last moment. He says there was no reason for this, but I suspect there was, and I feel more sympathetic now: we would have asked to visit the apartment, and it would have been embarrassing for him to refuse, and to tell us personally that he didn't even want us to enter the building. He also confirms what we'd heard when we were trying to acquire the rights to *If This Is A Man:* his mother, his sister and he had previously decided never to allow anyone to film or stage it. This is quite a shock to read in print. If we had known how definite their decision was – a rule, a blanket rule – would we have even tried? I'm obviously glad we did, and now it seems they are too. Not only have they heard good reports, but Renzo has read the reviews. He won't be able to come over and see the show, he says, but he hopes we meet one day.

And yes, he confirms he is named after Lorenzo (the man who saved his father's life in Auschwitz), and his sister's second name is Lorenza.

It seems that Primo thanked Lorenzo twice, for the existence
of both his children, writing his thanks into their names.

I send a reply to Renzo, thanking him in a friendly but formal
tone, echoing his own, and then I write a second, more personal
letter in my diary:

Dear Renzo,

I didn't mention my letters to your father. Without
knowing the whole story, it might have seemed weird to
you. But I wish you could know how much they helped me.
I really hope that we will finally meet. After your letter today, I have an image which I want to sketch during my next
Marietta session. It's of two shadows on either side of the
page, and two hands reaching out to greet one another.

With respect,
Tony.